Tl *Field* maga-zine is a remarkable phenomenon. For thirty years, these essays have appeared each week, for the last ten years from the pen of somebody known as Proteus. He now has a wide public following and his perception of the British countryside, of the manners and modes of her people, and occasionally of more cosmic matters has become the voice of a particular face of Britain. As such it has proved addictive reading, amounting in extreme cases – as the postbag shows – to a cult.

Proteus' inspiration from his native land is as much an ingredient of his writing as his wit and his accuracy in description. He writes of home details, the doings of friends and neighbours, of horses, dogs and birds of all species. He celebrates the soft south of England as well as the rugged north of Scotland.

THE CHANGING YEAR

THE CHANGING YEAR

Proteus *of The Field*

A selection from a decade of essays
presented by Wilson Stephens

London
UNWIN PAPERBACKS
Boston Sydney

First published in Great Britain in volume form by Frederick Muller Limited 1983
First published by Unwin Paperbacks 1985

UNWIN ® PAPERBACKS
40 Museum Street, London WC1A 1LU, UK

Unwin Paperbacks
Park Lane, Hemel Hempstead, Herts HP2 4TE, UK

George Allen & Unwin Australia Pty Ltd
8 Napier Street, North Sydney, NSW 2060, Australia

ISBN 0 04 910084 X

Made and printed in Great Britain by the
Guernsey Press Co. Ltd., Guernsey, Channel Islands.

Contents

About the Author

by Wilson Stephens formerly Editor of *The Field*

THE WRITER who calls himself Proteus guards his privacy carefully. His readers know nothing of him, except the internal evidence of his articles. The protection of this anonymity, on which his agreement to write in *The Field* is conditional, continues to be complete. One of its consequences are easily predictable. After ten years during which his essays have appeared every week without interruption, an increasingly large correspondence has centred upon them, and speculation about their authorship has become intense. But who he is remains as secret as ever.

As Editor at the time, I appointed him. As I also initiated the security measures which he requested, it has fallen to me to introduce this, this publication of eighty of his writings to celebrate his first decade. They have been chosen by the publishers in consultation with Mr. R. D. de Burgh Bingham, my successor in *The Field* chair. My role is not to make a critical assessment, but to outline the relationship of this very reserved man with a wide public which is no longer confined to these islands. To many thousands of people who do not know him, and will never know him, his perception of our countryside, of the manners and modes of her people, and occasionally of more cosmic matters has become the voice behind a particular face of Britain. As such it has proved addictive reading, in extreme cases a cult. In tracing these developments some comment is inevitable, but I begin with the historical background.

Proteus is the third contributor of the feature titled 'The Changing Year', and the first to use a pseudonym. By coincidence, at the time of writing he and his predecessors, both of whom are relevant to the emergence of Proteus, have all produced the feature over the same time-span, ten years each. The initiation of 'The Changing Year' therefore took place thirty years ago, in the second year of my editorship, in response to similarly-slanted articles in *Country Life* by C. S. Jarvis, the doyen and brightest star among country writers. Jarvis was then nearer the end than the beginning of his much admired tenure. In the unsentimental considerations of journalism, the time was ripe for a rival publication to provide a counter-attraction on whom his mantle might in due course fall.

My choice was the late Colonel J. K. Stanford, an experienced writer renowned as author of *The Twelfth and After* (the one good novel which, literary tradition has it, every writer finds within him, but which most of us are still seeking in vain). Stanford's journalism was distinguished by wide-ranging knowledge, and gusto which was occasionally sharpened abrasively. His distinction as an ornithologist led to the only interruption in his contributions when, as a member of an expedition studying bird migration, he spent some months in the Sahara. This commitment had been arranged before his engagement with *The Field*. Esmond Lynn-Allen ably deputised for him. At the end of a decade Stanford relinquished the post, having provided the forewarning necessary for me to find his successor.

An editor's eye must range freely in the eternal process of talent spotting. Mine had been caught by two short stories in *Blackwood's Magazine* over the initials C. B. That they were in *Blackwood's* at all was commendation bestowed on few; these, by their conciseness, structure, colour and insight were worthy of Kipling at his best. All that remained was to trace C.B. Coming events cast their shadow before, and what may sound simple proved difficult.

As was later to be my lot, the Editor of *Blackwood's* was duty-bound and honour-bound to protect the privacy of his contributor. My approach was repelled with what seemed stiff formality. This irritated me at the time, but stiff formality was to become a familiar weapon in my own hands when wielded in the opposite direction in years still far ahead. If C.B. had wished his full name to be known, I was told, he would have written under it. As he did not so wish, it would not be revealed. Letters would be forwarded, but C.B. was not notable for answering on this matter. Nor did he on that occasion.

However, there was a soft spot in his defences. One of his stories had marked him as a soldier of a mounted arm, and implied that he remained a serving officer. After long research in the Army List, and an equally long process of elimination, my attention focused on Brigadier C. C. L. Browne, of the Royal Artillery, in which regiment I had myself served. He qualified for the initials C.B. (among others) and, on direct inquiry, proved to be the man I sought.

Some small disquiet has affected me ever since, because the recruitment of Christopher Browne into journalism may well have diverted from the wider world of letters a writer possessing rare craftsmanship. Never from that moment, to my knowledge, did he write another line of fiction. What he did write ensures his place in the minds, and more notably in the hearts of his readers.

In contrast with the brusque declarations and robust humour of Stanford, widely appreciated though these had been or they would not have continued for ten years, Browne had an empathy which made him his readers' friend and gave him a special charisma. His quietly ironic and generous personality coloured his articles over the years and between the lines. The shadows of personal sorrow and failing health, kept strictly to himself, may have heightened their lustre by contrast. The knowledge that his life was unlikely to last long was with him throughout the last five years over which he wrote. For himself, he could dismiss that knowledge with soldierly contempt; for his family and friends he could not, but continued to provide spirited leadership until the day on which he sat down in his much-loved garden and saw it as his last view of this world. His readers, in thousands, felt his going as a personal loss. Without him *The Field* would be for ever poorer, many of them declaring him irreplaceable. Proteus had a difficult man to follow.

Now the veiled figure himself enters the narrative. Other

names will be mentioned, but only of men who have died. This is in line with the secrecy provisions on which he insisted when appointed. Not only was his name to be concealed, but neither affirmation nor denial was to be given if an inquirer sought to attribute authorship of his writings to any living person. In no way was the field of doubt, which surrounded him as a defensive measure, to be reduced; no process of elimination was to be applicable to him.

The death of Christopher Browne presented me with the need for two decisions. Without him, would 'The Changing Year' be worth continuing? If it were continued, who could write it? Conforming with the journalistic precept that matter is more important than men, and that successful features are immortal, 'The Changing Year' lived on. My chosen author assented in principle to my invitation, but stipulated absolute and permanent namelessness and concealment. This proviso, totally binding and difficult of implementation as it was, caused me to hesitate and to consult the chairman of *The Field*'s proprietorial board, Sir Geoffrey Harmsworth, himself distinguished as a writer of biography and travel, as a war correspondent, and as a very experienced publishing administrator.

He estimated the prospect of success by the person in question as sixty/forty; recommended provisional acceptance of the terms asked, and compliance over anonymity which he thought not worth arguing in view of the possibilities that the association might be short-lived; and that, if it were not, growing self-confidence might make the candidate 'less coy'. But he further predicted that the shock-effect of the change from Christopher Browne would be too great a handicap to be rapidly overcome, and that six months should be allowed for the new contributor to make the position his own, if he could. Meanwhile, no interim assessment should be made of his suitability. He should be left to sink or swim. We know the outcome.

The pseudonym, Proteus, was not self-chosen. His own suggestion was Crex, the Linnean designation of the corn-crake. Sir Geoffrey minuted adversely to this, on the grounds that phonetically and ornithologically it was too close to Strix (similarly, owl). The latter was used in *The Spectator* by the late Peter Fleming who at that time also contributed in his own name to *The Field*. Because my annual leave was about to start, and because the new contributor expressed no further interest in what he was to be called after his own proposition had been denied, the choice was left to Sir Geoffrey (the only person other than myself privy to the identity) and to my private secretary. Their aggregated knowledge of Greek mythology somewhat exceeded my own, and together they evolved Proteus. Their reasons were never explained to me; nor did their choice, which left an *après goût* of breakfast food, seem particularly inspired.

The point is significant in that for quite unrelated reasons Fleming happened to cease writing for *The Field* at that stage. So his name became conspicuous by its absence simultaneously with that of Proteus becoming conspicuous by its presence in the consciousness of readers. When, a year or so later, curiosity about the identity of Proteus began to grow, Fleming was the first to be credited with the series on the grounds of his previous association with *The Field* and known friendship with me. My undertaking prevented me from denying this. Fleming himself denied it, and was not widely believed. He was the first of many.

Meanwhile Proteus had taken time to form a rapport with *The Field* readership. All Sir Geoffrey's six months were needed for him to play himself in. His early articles, which were both tentative and explorative, were greeted with dismay. My own confidence was shaken. Giving what guidance I could, which was little enough, there were occasions when I wished the six months reduced to three. However, by the time they ended the issue had swung decisively towards Proteus. He had won his place, to my natural satisfaction.

Ever since, attempts to identify him have continued unabated. A situation has arisen analogous to that of A. J. Alan, the celebrated radio story-teller of the 1930s, a self-proclaimed pseudonym which was never penetrated. Many, however, were suggested as being 'the real A. J. Alan', including the late Duke of Kent, younger brother of Edward VIII and George VI. Innumerable people claimed to recognise the voice as that of an acquaintance or relative. So with Proteus, a High Personage has been cited as author of the essays on which that name appears. So have many others including politicians, media personalities and soldiers. I myself have been suspected. Many communities, from London clubs to southern villages, continue to claim one of their number as the unconfessed Proteus.

For reasons already stated, I have not been free to confirm or deny guesswork on the subject, and in that way to narrow the search. The security screen round Proteus remains unmodified. Three tiers of intermediaries stand between him and any attributable external presence. His letters are answered for him at third hand. The editorial staff of *The Field*, who prepare his scripts for press, know the route by which the material enters their sphere of action, but not where it originates. From this arises my status, comparable with that of Mr. W. H., the 'onlie begetter' of Shakespeare's sonnets, as the presenter of the ensuing essays. The difference is that Mr. W. H. was the mystery, his author well-known; in the case of Proteus, the reverse applies.

All that is publicly known of him is by exegesis from his writings. At first sight the image they present is vivid and seemingly close-up; looked at more critically, it recedes into a complex of unknown quantities, many of which end as glimpses of the obvious. It is difficult to say from what social bracket he writes. He seems to have a mind above politics. We know that he is a husband and father, hence male; that he fought in the Second World War, hence now about sixty years old; that his home is in Wessex; that he is a countryman, though he is not necessarily a farmer; that he has lived East of Suez, inferentially though not certainly in India. It is evident that his interests are outdoor, not indoor, inclusive of the life-style of earthworms and the majesty of God. In these and other ways he is no different from hundreds of conforming men. Some have claimed to see clues in his style – terse and not guiltless of syntactical eccentricities which some say a trained writer would avoid, and others say only a trained writer could survive. Thus the world sees faint outlines and colours of an elusive personality, occasional nuances but no more.

The significance of Proteus is not who he is, or who he is not, but how and what he writes. His eye picks up familiar details, explaining them into general truth or far-ranging possibilities. His is the art of the familiar in terms of the unexpected. Amid all the normalities of an English home, in an English village, in a county so English that not to name it seems natural, nothing that happens is abnormal, and all is within everybody's experience. Nevertheless the sensation is left, though never claimed, that something new has been discovered. The words are printed on paper; their effect is all in the mind.

His style is a mixture of verbal parsimony and vivid description. High literary circles would not call it elegant. But the staccato sentences of Saxon English each convey a picture, an arrested motion of country life, the sparseness of the words sometimes achieving a poetic intensity. It is as if fearing that words may stand between the reader and his meaning, he is determined that not even one too many shall be used.

Whatever the critics' views of these sharp, contrasting, evocative essays, there has been no doubt about their reception. Thousands of people, having read them once, have called for a version in book form. Here it is.

The essays have been chosen eclectically from a decade of British rural living, the end of which is materially and atmospherically very different from its beginning, and I have complied with the publisher's request to add introductory notes setting the background to the eleven chapters in which they are arranged, and some footnotes. These are printed in a type-face distinctive from that of the Proteus text.

WILSON STEPHENS
Clochan, Banffshire
August 1982

Time and Place

The theme throughout is Britain, the British scene, the British way, and British folk. But the face of Britain, however expressed, is in two dimensions. Nationwide and locally, time continually qualifies place; a single glance absorbs them both. First in panorama, then with feet on the ground, sometimes in his own vision and memory, sometimes through the eyes and speech of others, sidelights are thrown on the passing scene. Past and present come together. We are what we are because of what our forbears were. One of these essays, by containing a perhaps unguarded reference to the author's Shropshire upbringing, recalls from 'Wenlock Edge'

The blood that warms an English yeoman,
The thoughts that hurt him, they are there.

VIEW FROM ABOVE

EUROPE SLIPS EASTWARD beneath the homing aircraft. That last ditch, the Channel, once thought an impregnable obstacle, is traversed now in less time than athletes take to run a mile. Travellers cross it without knowing. But the ground below leaves no doubt whether it has been crossed or not.

Where Roman legions marched, and Gallic realism or Teutonic order now reigns, the topography speaks for itself. Roads run straight and intersect at right-angles. Fields and woods are square or rectangular. A rare parallelogram almost affronts the surrounding regularity. The countryside might have been laid out by Euclid. On the English side the view is very different. When the white cliffs fall behind our nation's character is printed on the land. It combines revelation with warning. English lanes wind crazily, sometimes responding to contours, sometimes contradicting them. Major roads swerve and swing, as if determined to miss their presumed objectives. Here and there signs of new highway construction reveal belated efforts to straighten them.

Between the roads the patchwork of crop, pasture and plough takes shape for which eccentric is the only word. If a jigsaw enthusiast carved up the landscape he could hardly make a better puzzle than generations of farmers and landowners have created. Small wonder that our mainland neighbours think us English mad. My sincere hope is that they long have cause to do so.

Hedgerows loop themselves round inexplicable appendices, like miniatures of the Dutch border at Maastricht. Some may think the original objective was to include a particular tree in a particular enclosure, and some may very well be right. Fields are any shape, and often there seems no reason for it. Outside the Fens, geometric patterns were evidently anathema to our ancestors, and remain so in our day.

A visitor's first aerial view of England must persuade him of the powerful English characteristic of individuality. The lie of the land is Nature's work. What is superimposed on it is a residue of the wishes and the obstinacies of generations who held fast to what they had. Ours is a landscape born from the conflicting interests of robust, sometimes bloody-minded men. When the land was theirs, they stood their ground. Neighbours were welcome to pursue their business, so long as they went round them, not over them.

Inconvenient as these attitudes may have been, there is for me much that is admirable in them. When practised (as they generally were) by men whose principle in life was to leave things better than they found them, the effect was to defend what had been gained by thrift against erosion by folly. They also reflected individual responsibility. For centuries no planning authorities, armed with a lien on other people's money, had yet replaced the feudal barons in deflecting the freedoms of ordinary folk. There was no compulsory purchase. Nor were there councils empowered to dissipate but unable to create, answerable corporately but not personally because their personnel is ever changing.

Whatever had been created was kept in being by its individual creators, their heirs or successors. The result was the richness of rural England and its villages. Even the profligacy of the present century has not obliterated this past, nor hidden it totally behind the present. As it progresses people grow increasingly aware of the worth of what we have inherited. Increasingly, too, steps are taken to see that it endures.

When the aircraft heads for Heathrow, the eye falls on Sussex. That sleepy-sounding county, an industrial zone reverted to rusticity, tells its own tale of reaction to the passing ages. A glance reveals how rews became roads, holding to the tortuous ways bequeathed by idiosyncratic countrymen and eventually imposing them on the motor age. They link villages sited by adventurers from Scandinavia and the German plain. After more than a thousand years of intervening exploitation by ironmasters and timber magnates, an eye above can still trace why those early settlers put down their roots in scattered hursts and greens which City men now call home. Vertical distance lends perception to the view.

Perhaps it leads also to the contrast between the European mainland and our island. Our gnarled individuality, the insistence on expressing which led to our ancient freedoms, may not combine easily with the readiness of others to accept the dictates of mensuration or even of logic. Thinking of the Common Market and of the supposed need to keep in step, one wonders what will happen to the aerial views. Which will alter, ours or theirs?

MARCH 1974

BELOVED OVER ALL

ENGLAND IS A confederation of shires. Englishmen think of the shire first, country second. Reminisce with an old soldier and he will tell you when he joined the Hampshires, the Warwickshires, or whatever else was his local regiment; he will not think of enlistment as joining the Army. A man plays cricket for Surrey and England, not for England and Surrey. Priority is clear. Our shire-before-country concept has parallels, but not rivals. Scots put clan first, nation second; had they not long done so, history would be different. Religion categorizes the Irish. Of the four nations of the British Isles only the Welsh put Wales first and inner divisions nowhere.

The county or, for those who prefer the English language as it was before new-fangled Latinization crept in with the Norman conquest, the shire polarizes English fidelity. Kipling knew the deep-rooted nature of his fellow countrymen so that for each of them 'one spot shall prove beloved over all'. For his own spot he named Sussex. Nothing less than a county would do. For an Englishman nothing more than a county matters. These lasting loyalties could not have been achieved unless each county had possessed a particular character imposing its own particular spell on the inhabitants. Those who first defined the shires knew them when they saw them, because England is in fact as well as theory a collection of contrasting regions.

Most of the shires had been formulated, their boundaries much as they are now, before the reign of Edward the Elder ended. He was son of Alfred the Great. In an island then thinly populated, almost unmapped, its few roads in neglect, it may be wondered how they did the job so well that it has lasted 1,000 years. I am in small doubt. They distinguished counties from their neighbours because they were and are distinct, as any sensibly observant man can see.

To test this, take them at random, visualize them one by one, and realize the differences. Somerset is Somerset because it is an entity sufficiently separate from the zones around it to require a name of its own. To this day only a fool would fail to know when he had left its lush alluvial land and entered red-soiled Devon, wooded Dorset, or the cold lean hills of Wiltshire. All three boundaries are as demanding of recognition as is the coast on the fourth side. Drive at dusk from Hertfordshire into Bedfordshire. It is obvious that there is a distinction; obvious, too, when one passes it. No county sign is needed to indicate where the clear Chiltern view is succeeded by a pearly mist above the clay.

County loyalty begins with topography and ends with a sense of belonging. We belong to counties, and they belong to us. The allegiance is not less real and just as indestructible for being bigoted as well as instinctive. To accept its force is less stupid than to deny it or to assume, as petty men have done, that the only significance of a county boundary is to decide where rates are paid. Dim in the miasmas of Whitehall, where files are the only reality, the transfer of Berkshire's white horse to Oxfordshire may seem something less than an enormity threatening broken heads in Wantage market place. Locally, it seemed very much otherwise.

The rolling stones among us acquire residential affinities, as it were, for counties other than our own. These seldom outweigh those conferred by our birth qualification. But they help us to see the hallmarks of counties to which we have no claim, and sometimes to realize the thorough good sense of those long-ago Saxons who saw them too, and drew the map accordingly. An administrator with enough eye for country to designate Northamptonshire would nowadays be unthinkable. This long, improbable crescent, swerving along its line of hills between the lowlands north and south, has a reality and a physical appearance which was positive enough to establish its identity in days when the people on the spot were the prime concern.

Nothing is English life comparable to counties has been so permanent, nothing so evocative of what each of us knows as home. To understand home one must leave it; and, of course, return. In the coming back counties call most strongly. Each to his own. Anywhere from Shropshire with silver on the oak boles, to Lincolnshire where kecksies swing in ceaseless wind, from Kipling's Sussex to the fells of Cumberland, the counties are small worlds of their own. Together they add up to England, when the need arises.

APRIL 1973

FAIR TO SEE

MY ARRIVAL HAS been in deep dusk, with a lacing of chill rain. So the view next morning came without forewarning, its breathtaking beauty a surprise bordering on shock. It was the best-named view in England, the Vale of Belvoir – Fair to See.

Beauty is in the eye of the beholder. It cannot be defined. It was enough for me, walking out from my host's house into that most subtle of all radiances, winter sunshine, to know that what met the eye was England. A Scot might have assessed it as no more than interesting evidence of agricultural practice. A visitor from Wales could be understood if he found it workaday and unimpressive in its lack of mountain grandeur. To me it was a manifestation not of Nature only, but of Man.

Little of England is as Nature made it. Most of it represents human use and adaptation by the passing generations. In Belvoir Vale they have handed down a gem of landscape and of living space to us. What we shall hand on remains to be seen. That early morning the quiet colours lay under a clear sky. Black hedges divided field from field, some the yellowing hue of clays, others a ruddier loam. The faint green of seeds was answered by the fading buff of stubbles spared from the plough by the long autumn drought.

The tawny bracken patches and olive green gorse balanced patches of whitening winter fog. Dark masses of wood and spinney contrasted with the pastel shades around them. Here and there the shining curves of a distant lane, wet from a night-long downpour, confirmed the swell of the land. Grey towered churches, spaced across the land, told where the villages lay.

This being truth, how could art portray it? I could think of no landscape painter able to capture and reduce to canvas this wide fresh scene, to imply the vigorous air rising from its breathing soil, and the damp touch of the breeze coming across it from fenland Lincolnshire. Perhaps Lionel Edwards, with his gift for awakening the sub-consciousness of outdoor folk, would get nearer than most. Imagination kept suggesting views of that flying patch of colour, with red dots behind it and on the flank, which sets the questions for foxhunters to answer. The lines across the hedgerows, so inviting from far off, would test nerve and heart in those who nowadays are better men than I. But, for all its fame, Belvoir Vale is much more than a hunting country.

In the first place it is home. Home to communities of people who have built their life-styles in the English manner. Not all of them are rich and influential, though some are. A comparatively small proportion, compared with the urban populations on their fringes, are members of trade unions with power enough to command listening senates. Most are unpretentious folk, living near if not off the land, accustomed to regarding governmental powers and practices as things remote and far away.

But now those powers are threatening them, their homes, and the way of life to which many have succeeded and others have adopted. The sort of life in which neighbourhoods matter more than picket lines, where people think of shops instead of supermarkets and boutiques, and few greatly envy the bigger money to be earned in different ways of life elsewhere, faces direct threat. So does the beauty of the Vale itself.

The National Coal Board seek Government consent to large-scale mining in the Vale. Among the comfortable words uttered to disarm local criticism has been the prediction that this would bring money to the area. Local reception has been less than universally favourable. No wonder. Money is not worth having at some of the prices asked for it. The sight of the Vale is enough to show what some of them may be. Meanwhile unanswered questions multiply. Thirty years ago we were told that nuclear power would supersede conventional sources of energy. Why has it not done so, and why mine more coal?

Miners' campaigns to prevent the closure of mines at which they work are familiar enough; so is the statement that some existing mines are kept open for 'social reasons' only. Why open more mines in districts with no existing mining labour force? North Sea oil has been hailed as the solution to Britain's energy problems, to some of our economic problems, and to the similar problems of some foreign nations. If so, who needs coal?

The truth is that we, and the rest of the industrial nations, are living as spendthrifts. We are burning up the world's reserves which by no known process can be replaced; releasing, at a rate which will exhaust them within decades, stores of energy which took many millenia to accumulate. In our life of unprecedented material ease and plenty the cry goes up 'Exploit! Exploit!' so that none shall go short – which means shorter than anybody else, however grossly the others are over-consuming.

What can it matter to vote-catchers, planners, and that corps of academic miscellania to whom a desecrated environment is the raw material of livelihood, that something of value should be lost? After all, they are in the reconstruction business. And perhaps they would prefer the world not to be too easily reminded of what England was like before their kind moved in, nor of what life was like when regard for the future kept a check on the rate at which the past was robbed to pay for the present.

January 1979

Later policy announcements suggest that disaster will not befall Belvoir Vale in the foreseeable future.

THE SPINNEY

For miles through a city's suburbs I had passed new houses, new streets, new shopping precincts, new roundabouts, new mounds of earth piled up by bulldozers and gleaming in the rain. Seeking clues to my destination, I checked the name board at each turning. Being also new, they stood out bright and clear beyond the swinging windscreen wipers. Crescents, closes, avenues and boulevards fell behind in steady succession. Then came one that was different in name but not in character. Almost heartlessly it was called The Spinney, not a tree in sight.

To ease the monotony, I turned into it. There was nothing to inspire. More red-brick, more piled earth, the same lowering grey sky and relentless rain. It was a cul-de-sac. A few seconds took me to the top. A U-turn took me out again. At least the digression eased the boredom, leaving something about which to think.

The Spinney, it had been called, but a less arboreal scene I never saw. Nothing but a few saplings tied to stakes, all their future before them, if the vandals held off, in giving some distant future leafiness to a long straight pavement. In one garden an incomer had quickly planted four apple standards, naked and only a yard or so high, shivering in the winter wind. Otherwise the area was as treeless as the Sahara. Yet The Spinney, that raw little enclave, would not have been so named for no reason at all. A real spinney must have stood there once. The memory lingered on in somebody's mind, and so did the name, to remind the inhabitants of the past nature of their patch of English soil.

Much countryside had been submerged as the city sprawled outwards; countryside which could easily be imagined. Meadows sweet with hay in summer, cornfields golden towards autumn, lanes blocked twice daily by calm-moving dairy herds. Where the clay-tinged water gurgled in new-dug drains had been brooks where moorhens fed.

The Spinney had been a hanger. On its slope, if centred on what was now the cul-de-sac's turning area, it could have dominated the landscape around it, catching the sun at dawn and dusk. Probably oaks were at its heart. This was neither elm nor beech country. The oaks would have been gale-tossed, stag-headed against two centuries of winters. Ash and hornbeam would have balanced their pattern, with hazel filling the sun-lit spaces between.

In spring Milton's rathe primrose and the wood anenome bloomed there in fresh drifts year by year until the bluebells and dog's mercury overwhelmed them. Then foxgloves came through, with spurge and nightshade to trap unwary blackberry pickers. Finally, after leaf fall, the stems of dogwood ruddy as a fox's pelt touched the drab winter scene with colour.

In summer, blackcaps sang there, shouting down the other migrant warblers. Longtailed tits lisped in the high branches and nuthatches performed acrobatics. Pheasants brought off their chicks and blackbirds demonstrated against tawny owls. Rabbits made the Spinney their base camp, pillaging the young corn in the fields around, and were in turn themselves pillaged by that grass-roots tiger, the stoat. Moles hunted the leaf-rich soil for brandling worms. Badgers came and went; perhaps some stayed.

The Spinney had been a living entity, self-contained yet part of the surrounding world, a tiny jigsaw piece in the expanse of England. Stirred by wind, nourished by rain, brought to life by sunshine and cleansed by frost, it was the product of English soil and English weather. Then, in a few short days, down it came, its trees crashing, its soil crushed and churned by vast weights and remorseless wheels, its living communities shattered and dispersed, as if it had never been, the place where it had stood being the only reality left.

The perpetuation of its name had seemed at first sight to be thoughtless insensitivity. I might have continued to regard it so had I not turned into the cul-de-sac which it has now become. My brief impression reminded me of the human occupants who had curtained themselves off on either side of their small road that led nowhere. The houses, though new and raw, were neatly pleasing. Their simple proportions gave them a Georgian air. And they were the houses of English folk. We English have a touch of genius for doing what is fitting, such as not overlooking the fact that we live in a place called The Spinney; a genius too for creating homes and gardens, and for improving the setting around them. Time would tell.

I shall not forget The Spinney. If I am fated to go that way again, five or ten years hence, I shall take the turning a second time. With its name as inspiration, the cul-de-sac will differ greatly from its appearance on that desolate and darkening day. There will, I think, be new trees growing, and birds will sing again.

JANUARY 1981

MONSTER IN THE LANE

AGAIN THE WOLF tree rears its ugly head. It was once a mighty oak. Lightning had blasted it long before it fell. Doubtless it stood upright for decades, drying and shrivelling in the wind, anchored with decreasing security by lifeless roots until some great storm laid it low. Down and out, it continues to resist obliteration. For longer than my lifetime it has lain on the broad verge at the edge of an unfenced wood. The stump of a snapped-off branch supports it, as if an old diehard were raising himself on an elbow for one last look at life. Each year it sinks a little further into the earth, and now the once great tree is almost prone.

In summer rosebay, bramble and nettle hide it. In winter, frost kills down the cover, so that the ancient presence comes in sight again. The weather has worked so long upon it that it becomes less and less like a tree at all. The lashing rain of the turning seasons, sunshine in blazing noons, clinging ice and driven snow have given it the frailty of old age, and the pallor too. Whitened now, and jagged, it looks like some lean beast crouching to spring on passers-by.

Inevitably our daughters called it the wolf tree, sublimating their fears by climbing over it in the Christmas holidays. Last week, rounding a bend in the lane, they saw that it had reappeared. Small wonder we speak of wolf-tree lane. Their friends have followed suit. When those friends, now children, have grown into grey village elders, and when the old oak has vanished, totally reclaimed by the soil which nourished it, wolf-tree lane will be common local parlance among a generation now unborn. Then, no doubt, diligent men from far away will engrave Wolf Tree Lane on an Ordnance Map.

It will not be a new story. Fanciful views of the twisted limbs of fallen trees, gleaming palely through a winter twilight or looming like monstrosities against a setting sun, must have given identity to many a Dragon Green, Headless Lane, Lion Hill, Ostrich Cross and Crocodile Corner, to cite a few. Deny it though we do, we are a poetic people. The bright imagery of children is immortalised for us in colourful names. To those in the know, reminders and check-lists are unnecessary. Conversely, he is a dull and unimportant fellow who remembers his neighbour's post-code.

Hunting countries are rich with the spoils of bygone small talk. To analyse it, even with local knowledge, is an intellectual exercise. Sometimes it is speculative, sometimes original research. At the former level Bee Furlong, Owl's Castle, Stew Pony and Frog Hall have exercised my mind. All have the freshness and incongruity beloved of youth. But this means little. A characteristic of the countryman is that he never grows up. Octogenarians keep their taste for schoolboy humour. Even diligent inquiry has failed to unlock the secret of Bowerman's Nose, on Dartmoor. Who is there with heart so dead that he can pass that primeval, upended rock without wondering who Bowerman was, what his nose was like, and what peculiarity of size, shape, hue or texture earned it this memorial? Somebody must know.

Tonight a north-westerly blows. Above torn clouds the stars are bright. Squalls alternate with moonlight which throws moving shadows from the tossing trees. Behind their headlamp beams the motorists know only the distinction between darkness and light. Those on their feet, as most men were when country lore was formed, see things differently. As place names grow, so do ghost stories.

Coming home across the fields a tall grey shape swayed soundlessly in front of me, suggestive of some priestly rite. A stranger, bursting thankfully into a local inn, might have told such a tale as would have established the presence of an unquiet spirit. I happened to know that trailing skirts of faded old man's beard hang from the top of a hedgerow at that point, even though I did not know until then what night can do to so everyday a sight.

NOVEMBER 1973

NOTHING SECRET

IN A CITY a man may lose himself and live unknown. The opposite applies in the country. There, in leisured tempo, a man can certainly find himself. But he must not be deluded into thinking that he lives unseen. Nothing he does goes unobserved. Around him at all times are keen eyes and keener brains. With the incisiveness of military intelligence, they read the evidence and draw deductions. Their conclusions filter mysteriously through the community consciousness and become common property.

'Well, we knew you'd been very busy,' one good lady remarked understandingly when I apologized for delay over the carnival programme. 'Lights on all hours. We sometimes wonder when you sleep.' So do I. But that is beside the point.

Much to the point is our own unsought but detailed knowledge of neighbours. If a lifetime has made one observant, the human race cannot be excluded from what one willy-nilly sees and hears. All countrymen can be assumed observant by habit. So what we know of other people's lives is likely to be greatly exceeded by what they know of ours. Hence the wisdom when out and about of assuming that all which is done is seen by somebody. The land has a thousand eyes. There are no secrets in it. An international crook could walk from Hyde Park Corner to the Royal Exchange, and back himself to go unnoticed. Not so on our down.

If a spaniel takes off on a hare, the gamekeeper will make a sly allusion next time we meet. If a horse leaves hoofprints on some seeds, the world will know whose horse it was. Conversely, the world soon learns who does not leave gates open, and who does. There is justice in the countryside's ceaseless vigilance. It also works both ways. For instance, I know the farm where plover's eggs were picked on a more than marginal date; what happened to a vixen and her cubs who kennelled in a rotten oak where two shoots meet; and who was where on the night the policeman's van was found with its tyres flat in a lane where no crime had been reported.

So it behoves us to walk in the paths of righteousness, whether legally defined or not. Commit an indiscretion, let alone a crime, and the truth will out. Concealment is possible only in crowded places. This is because a crowd has no pattern; no normality, departure from which denotes significance. When woodpigeons rise in a flock from the far side of a hill before I have reached the skyline I know that I am not alone. So I wait stationary for the next break in normality to lead me first to the direction, then to the identity of the intruder. Others do likewise.

A woodman straightens his back in time to see a hare come through. Whither it goes gives him a fair idea whence it came. Unless he is very deep in cover his eye will soon pick up who or what put it on its legs for an involuntary daylight journey. A tractor driver subconsciously scans the same view afresh whenever he turns at a headland, and rescans it consciously only when it differs. A moving man, a plume of smoke, cattle watching all one way, birds on wing in mass become his day's news. What lies behind will not escape him.

To me it is a comfort to lead an uncomplicated life in what inexperienced people would regard as rural seclusion. I know it to be a blaze of publicity, unobtrusive though this brand of limelight is. Thanks to it, none of us are far from friends. If the retired policeman down the hill did not appear at precisely half-past seven, clad in vest and braces, to empty a teapot on his compost heap, we should know that he was ill, and act accordingly. I know also that he, interpreting some privately categorized signs in the opposite direction, would do the same for me. Such is life. For others, where the long streets roar, there would be no caring of that kind. Submerged in mass activity, the need would pass unnoticed. Such in existence.

JULY 1974

END OF A DAY

WESTWARD THE DOWNS rolled themselves away in grey-green ridges, like a swelling sea. Black shadows marked the valleys. Beyond, a choleric high summer sun was soon to dip. By my own toil, before the night, the scene had a sense of ceremonial. Four acres of hill-top hay, hand-turned three days before, now lay in windrows ready for the baler. It was not a lot, but some.

Every little helps this year, when hay is as gold in Klondyke, and men ready to stake their claims on roadsides, playing fields, churchyards and village greens. So the family mobilized and won with minimum mechanical aid the cut from two small closes. By so doing we added our small quota to the summer's fruitfulness, and the result of our labour was a sight worth seeing.

It was also one of those sights which puts time in its place. Because it is a universal human activity, haymaking unites a man with all other haymakers down the ages. Ours, perhaps, were the 2,000th windrows to lie on that little close. King Alfred's Englishmen, only a few generations removed from Saxons, would have known the truth of it. The same sun going down across the same billowing landscape, the same chill evening air, the same sense of duty done in the continuation of life, the same blisters, the same sunburn, the same thirst, told them and us alike that work is the salt of the earthly pilgrimage.

There would have been minor differences, of course. Our prongs are tempered steel, theirs were wooden. They might have felt that a beaker of mead would not come amiss. We had other plans. In my case it was, first, to walk the top hedge again. Work well done cannot easily be left; always there is another finishing touch. A further truss or so was conjured from the reach of brambles with the ease of a skill reborn. For now I was almost disembodied, a spectator of myself in action. Four days earlier the prong had been a non co-operator, rebellious in my hands, making me its slave. Then the rhythms of a forgotten task came alive again, wrists worked together instead of in opposition, balance returned, weight went automatically to the correct foot, so that I became the prong's master, and the swath turned with little effort. New ease freed the mind to think those cosmic thoughts which normally come on long uneventful days with a salmon rod. How long since I first made hay? Really made it, as distinct from pitching-up the bales, or doing the dude's job on the tractor seat? There would be no change out of two score years.

We led with horses then. I am not sorry they have been made redundant. The picture was idyllic, the truth otherwise. The elder sprays we twined in the bridles did too little to reduce torment by flies through long hot days with interludes of sweating toil. Men sweated more than horses, of course. No chance for them to be unhitched to stand in the shade of elm or oak. They worked on until women arrived with sandwiches, and almost any long drink except cider, from which wise men steer clear in the heat of the sun.

Two of my own women had been dutiful aides in the enterprise. Light was failing now. From the far end of the field came a flick of movement from a summer dress and a child's far-away voice, cutting across the centuries in the mood of the moment.

'Mummy is this what Ruth was doing, Ruth in the Bible?' came the penetrating timbre of junior daughter.

'No dear, Ruth was sickling corn.'

'What's sickling corn?'

The two figures walked slowly up the field. From behind me, senior daughter spoke. Characteristically she had materialized from nowhere with claims to one-upmanship. 'How many slow worms have you seen? I've seen three. And there's a partridge's nest in the hedge; you can stroke the mother bird, she won't go away. Did you know about the rabbits? There's lots.' She is one of those at whose approach wildlife lines up to be introduced. Hay, however, remains conspicuously unmoved. It seemed not the moment to discuss productivity norms.

My wife had a basket. She would. 'Will you have your cold tea now?' she asked. I hope King Alfred's English would not turn in their graves, but the answer was Yes. 'I'm having a long weak whisky,' she said 'and there's orange squash for those who want it.' We lightened the basket.

'The sun's quite gone now,' said senior daughter. 'Is that an owl?' Apart from which it was a quiet walk home down the hill to the quiet sleep of those who have made hay.

JULY 1975

The rain in May that fills the grasses did not fall that year.

VOICE OF THE PEOPLE

MEN WITH PURPLE faces stand beside their boards and lace the winter air with message. 'Sixes the field', 'Tens bar two', the raucous syllables bubble and seethe, fusing themselves into a chorus which quickens my blood. It is the voice of Mammon. Tattersall's and the Silver Ring are in full cry.

Not for me the mirage of easy money. Each of us, it seems, feels impelled to stand aside from some activity enjoyable to others. I opt out of betting. It wastes time, especially at the races, where I go to see the horses. But as sonic background, betting's brazen uproar expresses elemental England. At the heart of it simple men pursue simple aims. They are well content to do so without hectoring their neighbours, nor minding other people's business. Their swelling incantations rank high among collective outdoor sounds.

The hubbub on the rails is as much a voice of the wild as hound music and the clamour of migrating geese.

Curiously, we who listen diligently to the sounds of Nature give little heed to humanity's communal cries. Knowing the meaning, and so lacking the bait of mystery, we take them for granted. On this mild westerly day my window is open. No chime is needed to tell me the time is 10.30. High-pitched, free cries announce that the schoolchildren are in the playground.

Midway between song and shout, the sound of newly released pre-adolescents resembles nothing in the world except the same sound in the next village, and in the village after that. From Land's End to the Border, each playground chorus is identical. There is no telling what words are uttered. They cannot all be the same. But the cadence is. Borne on the breeze, or echoed across a valley, the voice of a playground is as English as a peal of bells, and as recognizable. Unknowingly I must have helped to produce it in my time. Now, meeting my village contemporaries and noting their thickening build, the primeval voice of the schoolboy seems to link generation to generation.

Some dutiful fellow should analyse the sound patterns of playgrounds, nation by nation. Life is full of lost opportunities, and I have missed my widest chances to listen and observe. It is an intriguing thought that the playgrounds of the world may repeat in addition to English freedom the melody of Celts, the *panache* of France, the solemnity of Teutons and the rhythms of the Slavs.

Not in conglomeration only does the human voice become idiomatic. It can do so without an understandable word. Some solo performances rivet attention. The richest sources seem to be the worlds of sport and of formalized salesmanship.

A well-travelled man who, in the English winter, fancies he hears a Frontier agitator haranguing a mob in Pushtu can be quickly assured of the truth. It is that a huntsman is cheering his hounds as they draw. What he says is plain enough to foxhounds; the way in which he says it distorts it for human ears as surely as a scrambler renders strategic discussions secret.

For years I have tried to detect a word of meaning from the hearty-looking men who, with downcast eyes, appear to mutter rapid prayers in northern market-places. They are, of course, selling sheep. And somebody, of course, is buying them, which accounts for occasional abrupt cessions in the liturgy. But who, and at what price, cannot be detected.

If the marketing of sheep is, at the moment of truth, almost a *sotto-voce* matter, the same transaction over fish seems very different, but equally mysterious. Fish auctioneers tackle their task with maritime vigour, pitching their voices against the screams of sea-gulls over the dock as if pronouncing a ceremonial curse. I have a private theory that these proceedings are conducted in Latin, if only because I have yet to recognize a word of English in them. But they could not be conducted by any but Englishmen in English ports. The English voice and the English manner is even more distinctive than English speech.

The modish thinkers will one day finish writing-off our national character. The continentalizers must eventually exhaust their efforts to wipe out any characteristics which make Britain different. And then our fidelity to our own ways will declare that imitation of the universal is not an obsession after all among Englishmen.

FEBRUARY 1974

TALK AT TWILIGHT

EVENING FELL AFTER a long warm day. It being spring, when there is much to be done, there were warm thirsty men to greet it. They had forgathered at the inn and when time was called they did not at once go home. They stood in the forecourt, gostering. From my garden the sound was clearly audible, spreading its comfortable message to the night that here were talkative and friendly fellows. Coming in from my last rounds, I reported the sound of gostering to my wife. She, reared in the sophisticated atmospheres of the Punjab, Salisbury Plain and Aldershot, did not understand the word. And realization dawned that I had spoken out of the past.

The verb to goster entered my vocabulary in early youth, from Shropshire. I cannot remember when and where I had last heard it used. But there is no doubt what it means. It refers to that low burble of conversation from cronies enjoying a private chat, erupting periodically into loud masculine laughter which promptly subsides. My grandmother, a serious-minded and purposeful woman, held gostering in disapprobation and spoke of it in withering terms whenever she heard it. To her it signified light-headedness and time-wasting. Additionally her sweetness of disposition never quite overcame the commonly held feminine delusion that when men laugh the motivation is apt to be indelicate.

Knowing better, my memories of gostering are second-hand. To goster at all, one's voice must have broken, and by the time mine had done so we had moved out of gostering country. So it was always as an eavesdropper, never a participant, that I remember those gatherings of shirt-sleeved men in the gloaming at cottage gates or at the tap-room door, and the manly, far-carrying rumble of voices.

In those days, the first decade after the First World War, men gostering on one side of the village could clearly be heard on the other. Not the exact words, of course. The rolling rustic vowels fused together to convey the spirit of what was being said, but hid its exact significance. What mattered was that good human speech was about the loudest sound in the countryside at dusk. The thunder of aircraft and the revving of cars did not drown it then. The comings and goings of neighbours were signalized by their tones and accents, not by their engine notes. The banalities of television had not mesmerized the community and excluded conversation. So there was much enjoyable gostering on summer evenings, when the day's work was done, especially if the weather was puthery.

That word dropped out unbeckoned in the slipstream of gostering. It, too, came, from long ago, and from Shropshire, although I hear my well-travelled mother use it unselfconsciously when occasion demands. Weather becomes puthery when thunder is about, clouds hang low, the air grows heavy with heat and damp, flies swarm, thoughts turn to making cottage cheese, and ale is called for after sundown.

Counties have their own words and phrases. Since most are onomatopoeic and reflect the experiences of ordinary folk, they are among the most expressive in the language. They long had their place as local status symbols. Not to know them was an admission of being an off-comer. Now the greater mobility of life and the reduced influence of work on the land, which rooted families in villages, have caused a wider interchange of words. Greater literacy and more general communication hastens the process. First the cinema, then the radio, released into our language a great influx of transatlantic words, phrases and constructions. The English most of us now hear has an Esperanto quality within the context of Anglo-Saxon, being universally comprehensible throughout this kingdom and America.

My heart still warms to dialect. It is a natural manifestation of the independence of Englishmen, of their refusal to conform to a common pattern. Long may we retain this. And of course dialect was stronger and more important, when, for me, the world was young . . . when roads were dusty, villages self-contained, isolated except on Fair days, and entertainment came from neighbours instead of an electronically fitted box. It was a good time to be alive. And so is this. Doubtless somewhere, far away from where I write, men still goster in the Severn vale.

MAY 1973

Home Details

An Englishman's home is his castle (equally so are the homes of the Scots, Welsh and Irish). Proteus, a very evident Englishman, writes graphically of his. Not much is made known of its structure, appearance and contents; we are left to imagine them. He is concerned with the life within and around it – the life of himself and his family, the impact of the neighbourhood, the never-forgotten presence of its unofficial residents, even the fortunes of its guardians against rough weather, the trees.

PLACE OF ASSEMBLY

IF THE POSTMAN, the rector, the girl groom, the gamekeeper's daughter and the schoolmaster's brother are gathered together to drink coffee with the lady of the house and discuss the Common Market, the choice of carnival queen, the incidence of smoker's cough, or anything else, several propositions may be taken for granted.

They are likely to be in our kitchen. If they are not, they will be in somebody's else's kitchen. And if they are indeed in somebody else's kitchen, then others forming a similarly mixed company will be in our kitchen, socializing. For that, as much as preparation of food, is what country kitchens are for. He is an imprudent man who imagines, as I did, that he can nip in with his breakfast tray, leave it, and go about his business. If he has any such ambition he should pause outside the door, and if he hears a burble of voices, retreat pussyfoot. Otherwise he will shortly find himself burbling too, and to disengage from burbling is no light matter.

Having naïvely walked in and found the company assembled as stated, thus becoming trapped, it was interesting to disentangle the ostensible from the true reasons for the presence of each coffee drinker. Experience has made me a realist. So discrepancies were to be expected. They were illuminating.

The rector, a poor liar by clerical standards, had just dropped in because he had not run across us lately. A likely tale. In fact, he had seen that the lady of the house was next on the roster for church flowers, and wished to discover if the operation had yet reached the planning stage. She has never actually failed in her duty, but she is apt to leave her effort as late as Harry Wragg the jockey used to do. The girl groom is there because she has a nose like a pointer. She can wind a brew of coffee at 60 yards, and did. So she came to ask whether the saddle cloths are out of the Bendix yet. If they had not been, there would have been time to put them in, switch on, rinse them, dry them and iron them before she stops speaking for the rising generation.

The postman is there because he had a package too large for the letter box, so had to ring. He would have been there even if he had not had to ring. All suspect that without this routine fortification of his energies, he would flake out before the next house. The gamekeeper's daughter has arrived for professional reasons. She stumps the country setting, perming, and in other ways refurbishing the crowning glory of every belle for miles. Be there a dance or a dinner party her book must be made up far in advance, and subtle are the stratagems employed to secure the latest possible appointment.

The schoolmaster's brother specializes in discovering urgent jobs on other people's property. As, for instance, the blocked ditch about which I had done nothing, well knowing that in the fullness of time he would. So he came in the guise of a supplicant wondering whether I could spare a few Christmas Drumheads as a lead-in to a discussion on recompense.

Whatever their purpose none could have been present had they not possessed qualifying status. To define this is impossible. Kitchen coffee coteries are not composed on the principle of too grand or not grand enough. We have had the Lord Lieutenant in ours, not because he is the Queen's representative, but because he is on the network. The doctor's wife will not gain admittance in a thousand years. The police superintendent will be jovially received, but only in the study. A great cohort of leading ladies are drawing room material, and nothing more.

Yet there are the self-elected many who confidently enter that great crucible of human quality, the kitchen. There they open their hearts, and indeed their mouths, debate issues great and small, and ensure that fingers are kept on the pulse of public affairs, and private ones too, for miles around. Happily we are on other networks, also. To be received by friends at their front door, except on a formal occasion, would be chilling. We go as of right to the kitchen. And we are not alone.

Country kitchens, warm, spacious, friendly, the air fragrant with rising dough and roasting chickens are the club rooms of the rural cognoscenti. And not of them alone. They have become, as it were, the brood chambers of the households in a manner impossible in the days when green baize doors preserved the caste system. Even as I write, there steals upon the ear a familiar and imperious voice. 'Lunch will be served,' it declares *animoso*, 'when there's room to work in the kitchen. So get out – now!' And there emerges, unabashed, a file of offspring and their boon companions, ears cocked for sounds of a follow-up by the dumb-waiter.

JUNE 1975

HEARTH AND HOME

YEARS HAVE PASSED since we kept our home fires burning to any noticeable extent. Recognition that households are now do-it-yourself, anyway for most of the time, impelled new methods. Mechanization replaced departed personnel. We mechanized cooking, cleaning, laundry. It was natural to mechanize heating too.

To light a fire has been a top-level decision for a decade. The gain in cleanliness is great, thanks to the absence of airborne ash which falls as dust on every surface. Combustion is far away, in the boiler room, its warmth efficiently distributed. We had not mourned the naked flame. Fuel also arrives efficiently, pumped in every six months or so from a great tanker which comes and goes without fuss, by men who never leave gates open. On the whole it has arrived economically too, for few of us cost accurately the alternative price of wood and coal. The time consumed in persuading the merchant to deliver, or in implementing a market economy over the purchase or cutting of wood, and the effort (even if one's own) in fetching and carrying, should all be parts of the calculation.

We were glad to be spared them, and the most we ever said was 'Nice to see a fire', or words to that effect, when on high day or holiday, or in honour of guests, the smoke went up the chimney once again. We had parted from a centrepiece of family living immortal for a million years. We had dispensed with rites of lighting and tending symbolic as well as practical since man first came to terms with fire. The ease with which we had done so was remarkable. Of course we were not alone. Most of those who read this article will have done likewise, or been party to the doing. Now when oil prices rise, the pound falls, and exploitation of local resources becomes a natural response, we shall not be alone in modifying the policy, and using old-time warmth to reinforce the new.

Those of us who have abandoned open fires now face reunion with them. They may be welcomed back as absent friends or accepted as dire necessity. Probably the latter will be the majority verdict. None of humanity's traditions can have been more thoroughly or more swiftly abandoned. Hearth and home has ceased to be a familiar concept. People still declare, as if scraping the barrel for something favourable to say about the object of a diminished affection, that a fire gives a room a focal point. I doubt even that. The cynosure of every eye is now the television set.

My personal complaint against the once-loved British fireplace was its wastefulness. Not only the smoke went up the chimney; much of the heat went, too. Those living in more rigorous climates look with sympathetic wonder at our fireplaces, mostly sited at floor level where they warm only the ankles thoroughly, and the anatomy above the belt scarcely at all.

In Norway pot-bellied stoves six feet high and built of brick like gigantic, thermodynamic Toby jugs, dispense heat waist-high, and are designed to prevent it leaking away. I once asked a resident in Finnmark, far north of the Arctic Circle, how he stayed warm in the winter. He indicated first his stove then, from the window, great log piles of birch and fir. In terms not less explicit for their Nordic frankness, he declared, 'Ve haf not cut up all zis vood to varm ze arses of ze seagulls'. His words returned to mind with the cash-saving prospect of log fires again, and appropriate action followed. The posteriors of our avian neighbours, which occasionally include seagulls, shall derive minimum comfort. Our dining room fireplace, conceived in bygone ages, and extended, modified, improved, complicated, and rendered increasingly hideous by successive generations of our predecessors, has been demolished.

Standing in the space which formerly it filled, I gazed at the vastness of the central chimney, and the beauty of its brickwork, upon which the eye could not normally fall. It was big enough to take a small car. The great gape of its mouth, so high above through which the stars looked down, explained why combustion at blast furnace intensity had been needed to produce an effect on the room in which it burned.

News travels fast in the countryside. Every inhabitant of the village, and some from a wider area, soon knew what was afoot. On their cumulative recommendation much of the chimney has been blocked in. Meanwhile some of our trees are down. Others must be felled. The stutter of a chain saw will be the prelude to fires. They are to be looked forward to; as also, though with less enthusiasm, is the clearing of the ash. My private hope is that the need will have passed by the time our windfall wood is burned, and that there will not be many open fires. They have their time, and their place. These are not the present, nor my house.

Camp fires far away, round which we sat blanket-wrapped and carefree when tomorrow was another day, if it ever came; dignified fires in English houses, flames flashing on polished irons and shining brass, glass screens to deflect the heat, a professional eye for ever on them; such things belong to days gone by. We live differently now. I am glad the blazing hearth may burn in welcome to our friends. For ourselves I am content to set the time-switch according to our needs, to take the ease and let the tradition go, as often as I can afford.

NOVEMBER 1976

THE NORTH VOID

HISTORY IS FULL of instances in which previously neglected territory becomes of strategic significance. History repeats itself. 'What this place needs,' declared the lady of the house, 'is a decent box-room.' She spoke in that pithy way which ladies of houses adopt when approval is sought for something which they regard as a foregone conclusion. I waited to hear more. I soon heard it.

'There's all that wasted space over your dressing room,' she continued. 'It goes on over your bathroom and your end of the corridor as well.' Her statement produced mixed feelings.

The recurrence of 'your' could have left a guilt complex on a conscience less clear than mine. It must be taken purely as expressive of locality, I told myself, and not to imply, however remotely, that my selfish interests were a stumbling-block to the full exploitation of our domicile. But the words which really rankled were 'wasted space'. Here was a fine way to refer to a romantically named area of my possessions, so inaccessible that in 10 years of ownership I had never yet visited it. However, I was aware of its existence. The surveyors, two roly-poly men, had wriggled and squirmed through a hatch in the corridor ceiling before we bought the house. They had returned safely, recorded their impressions briefly, and marked it on their plans as the Romans marked Ultima Thule on maps – not in expectation that anybody would ever go there, but to indicate zones beyond mortal ken.

Not for them so contemptuous a term as 'wasted space'. They talked and wrote, as surveyors do, in Churchillian rhythms implying far-flung perspectives. Their report revealed that when contracts were exchanged I should become possessed, in addition to all else, of the North Void. And now, change and decay in all around I see, the North Void was redesignated as merely idle cubic footage. Farewell to all its undertones of frozen wastes and echoing distances, and perhaps even the ghosts of trolls. It was to be, and indeed has since become, a decent box-room.

The local builder and his mate wrought the transformation. For fifty pounds, and rather more cups of tea, they enlarged the hatch, strengthened the floor, fitted a cantilever ladder, and anchored a rachet-hoist to winch up heavy objects. As a prelude to signing the cheque, I was invited to view the consequences.

Whatever the North Void once had been, it was now unmistakably a box-room. Already it had assumed the rôle of shrine to the household gods. Its dim religious light fell on items which had been dear to others and, by their presence there, were in their fashion dear to us. Canvas trunks, their green long faded by the Indian sun, bore the stencilled names of forebears who had travelled Port Out and Starboard Home. Framed samplers testified the virtue of pale little girls for whom Sir Robert Peel was Prime Minister. A set of golf clubs, dimly recollected as my own, reminded of the follies we commit when young. A doll's house, already abandoned by the rising generation, bespoke the passage of time. The family high-chair stood smugly by, waiting recall to duty.

And yet there were absentees, without which no box-room can be passed as really decent. We have no rocking-horse to stand wildeyed for ever, while the spiders be-web its flaring nostrils. No disused croquet set, the other *sine qua non*, is available for storage yet; if there breathe folk with hearts so dead that they can disuse a croquet set, we are not among them. No primeval gramophone. No ancient sewing machine. No mercifully abandoned ukulele.

Even so the box-room has been established as a threshold of history. The cantilever ladder re-elevated itself with smooth efficiency. The hatch cover descended in its place. I turned my back on the static scene beyond them. So ended my only visit to what had been the North Void. Figuratively speaking it will not have been my last. As the dust settles, as it does in all decent box-rooms, it must eventually fall on something which, by being often in my hand, will have qualified as part of me.

Strange-clothed, odd accented descendants, exploring there in years to come, will find my salmon-gaff, an ancient ice-axe, perhaps a cartridge bag, and, puzzled, speak my name again. It is in box-rooms, rather than by storeyed urn and animated bust, that most of us are destined to be remembered. Though the point is of no consequence, even to me, I prefer the North Void.

FEBRUARY 1975

Times have changed. Much more would be needed to finance the job in 1983.

OPEN DOORS

WHEN WE GO away my wife leaves a note for the burglars. It says that the silver is in the bank, and so are unspecified valuables. Her purpose is to save industrious fellows the toil and sweat of wrecking the place in search of what is no longer there. This pre-departure rite has my admiration. To see in one's partner such fidelity to detail, not to say consideration for others, makes glad the heart of man. Yet for long it seemed a belt-and-braces operation. Now my opinion is modified.

An excessive luminance on the inner door of the porch greeted me on two mornings this summer. I am habitually first down. The brightness of the frosted glass had only one explanation. The outer door had been left open and the light of a new day was shining through. Since the silver was present and burglars absent on each occasion no harm had been done. This was special relief since the door could have been left open only by me. I am habitually last up. Nevertheless, my mind had its forebodings.

Drinking a first cup of tea, I tut-tutted to myself as heads of households do when something untoward has occurred. Presumably we might have been murdered in our beds, less remote a contingency than it was before 'If in doubt act soft' became the policy of successive Governments. Perhaps the note for the burglars should be provided every night, and make the extra point that nothing upstairs is worth taking. Then at least we could sleep peacefully through any malfeasance.

The significance of this mild anxiety eventually dawned upon me. What was remarkable was that it should be felt at all. In the 1950s nobody bolted doors, and seldom even closed them from May to September, in my home village. Day and night they stood open. Nobody worried. Nobody intruded. Nobody stole. Such was then the climate of life in the English countryside. We assumed that not only our neighbours, but all who might come and go, were honest. Experience did not prove us wrong. To have locked a door would have implied otherwise, made us feel uncomfortable, and left us wondering against whom we turned the key.

The open door was the symbol and result of faith in each other. It was also the channel of communication. How else would the sexton retrieve the key to the belfry from the rectory cloakroom? Or the Calor gas man change the cylinders? Or the postman pick up the outgoing letters? Or the gardener water the conservatory plants? The ever-open doors permitted people to go about their business, and their pleasures, knowing that life would go on too. There was no waiting for others. Nor was there a hectic rush to be on time. Nobody would suffer by half-an-hour's delay. What was needed would be done in a man's good time, and hence in good humour. All could come and go as and when they liked.

An Englishman's home was and is his castle. But defence was unnecessary as recently as that. Things are changed. Keys and bolts are needed now. Perhaps moat and portcullis, or their equivalents, will be needed next. But let us hope not. And I believe not. Incontrovertibly we were recently a great people. No doubt assails me that we still are, though the evidence has been submerged for lack of familiar outlets for our qualities. Among the things which made us great was team spirit. We were Britons, and aware of what this meant. 'Come the four corners of the world against us' was not an empty phrase. Its legacy permeated everyday life. Those who live thus do not steal from comrades. More of us felt comradeship then than feel it now.

It was our habit then to think of our united interests. What benefited Britain would in the end benefit all. It had not become fashionable to stress, and if necessary create, fission between sections of the people. Honesty was a national asset, and anything else was unworthy of us. Since then the crime rate has soared. One day we British will exercise our commonsense, which though latent, never fails. Then we shall cease listening to the muddleheads who pretend that larceny is a social evil for which those who do not steal are in some way as much to blame as those who do. Instead we shall recognize again the old good habits which enabled us to live happily together with ever-open doors.

SEPTEMBER 1973

FAMILY GROUPS

SOMEBODY PUSHED A large, heavy, stiffbound book towards me and said: 'Remember these?'. I was visiting kinsfolk seldom met and it was, of course, a photograph album. More graphic than a graveyard in its evidence of mortality, more explicit than the calendar in measuring the strides of Father Time, to turn its pages crystallised thoughts about cameras and the dubious part they play.

Embattled aunts of yesteryear, immobilised for ever on settees, sat shoulder to shoulder, proclaiming their generation. Lace and satin still endured on summer afternoons in the inter-war years; gorgets encircled senior necks, supporting in the case of widows (such being then the custom in our old-fashioned family) gold-encased miniatures of the departed. Hair was piled upwards in symmetrical outlines, like domes on a Russian church.

Uncles leant upon each other, heavily moustached and straw-hatted. Their faces had the cadaverous look which overmuch hair about the lips and below the ears has also given to the present generation. Some, photographed at their favourite summer recreation, grasped cricket balls in threatening attitudes. Not a smile among them. The ladies stared in frosty dignity, their menfolk glowered at the camera – as, in my opinion, well they might. For the camera is a deceiver, distorting its records of the passing scene, constantly mocking that aphorism which says it cannot lie.

It does, nearly every time the shutter clicks. For life is a continuing process in which people and scenes continue too, never being complete or static, and the camera cannot capture continuing truth. All it can do is to freeze what existed as transient truth for one-fiftieth of a second or much less, preserving it for ever as if it had permanent validity. We all know that it had nothing of the kind. An artist with insight into human nature, and the skill to combine it with the pictorial exactitude of a portrait, can achieve truth. But the camera cannot interpret. We have to accept its evidence of a passing moment as being total truth.

Those representatives of a generation now no more, typecast for ever in that particular album, doubtless look perfectly natural to those who never knew them. Only for those of us who did know them is the discrepancy apparent. Their immobility, so foreign to them all, leaves them as little resembling their true selves as the pillar of salt resembled Lot's doubtless winsome wife. When they rose from their settees, or actually played cricket, they were robust and active people. Foxhunters all, and full of strange oaths when heated in the chase, they left rousing and vivid memories of themselves. The camera diminishes them to lifeless, set features amid the encircling sepia. The great liar understated its subject as usual.

Hence I excuse myself from enthusiasm for family groups and that often awful thing, the snapshot. Freedom from them is increasingly difficult to achieve. Not only is the setpiece – which, being proclaimed in advance, gave opportunities for evasive action – less in favour, but there are more cameras about nowadays.

The modern young acquire their first cameras at the age of about eight. More remarkably they also acquire the not inconsiderable financial subventions which permit films to be bought and developed. And the fashion now is not to line up aunts on settees, bidding them to comport themselves with due restraint, but to stalk all relatives of whatever seniority as if they were wild creatures, and photograph them when offguard. So all life is apt to become a camera safari.

Not even such humdrum occasions as tea on the lawn are exempt. And afterwards comes the bitter harvest. What the camera disgorges varies between those aspects of arrested motion which reveal one as less photogenic than previously, or which give grounds for hilarity in which it is seldom possible to join wholeheartedly.

Even if, as sometimes happens, no pictures 'come out' the clicking and whirring of modern photography is less than welcome. My attitude to technology is that if it must be endured, at least it should keep silent. An additional pity is that photography gives its questionable blessing to oddities of behaviour which do not improve the social scene.

The presence of a casual photographer, generally a hanger-on such as the escort of a favoured niece, soon declares itself. No matter to whom the young man has been introduced, he is magnetised away to the windows side of the room or, if outdoors, upsun so as to get the stronger light behind him. Hardly is he there than the light-meter reading, clicking and button-pressing begins. If the party has any sense of occasion about it, there may well be more than one of them. They hop around in crouching positions, each with one eye closed, squinting upwards. 'Must get the angle,' they mutter. I have yet to see the necessity.

Far be it from me to mar the simple joys of others. In that worthy cause I shall continue to allow myself, my family, my possessions and other personal aspects of life to become the subject of album browsers the length and breadth of the land. The fact remains that when camera-danglers cross the threshold, I simply wish they would go away.

October 1980

MOMENT OF DEPARTURE

IF THE STERLING fellows who put racehorses into starting stalls ever seek alternative employment I can offer a suggestion. Their skills would come in handy at loading my family into a car. As a warm-up exercise before Flat racing re-starts, their assistance might even be of mutual benefit.

Whether other heads of households suffer similarly, or whether I am exceptional in being thus afflicted, I do not know. The fact remains that to reach a situation in which one wife and two daughters are all aboard simultaneously is for me a process demanding resource, patience and, above all, luck. It resembles on a larger and more fraught scale that maddening Christmas puzzle which requires three ball-bearings in a little transparent case each to be seated in its own recess. To inveigle one of them into place tests skill and guile. A steady hand and a cool nerve may eventually see the second safely home. And there, with the distaff side as with ball bearings, is the rub. To install the third presents in itself no greater problem, but in the meantime one of the first two will have hopped out.

Hence my idle dream that a brace of intrepid chaps might link hands round the sterns of my ladies and, with the requisite manly heave, propel them willy-nilly into the vehicle. Such a technique would provide more force and positive effect than mere importunings, threats, and cajolery can achieve. But it would not be enough.

Once a horse is in a starting stall only the Starter lets it out. Put spouse or offspring into a car, and the doors on the other side constitute much-used escape hatches. They would need to be picketed, at the cost of extra man-power. As it is, feminine manoeuvrings at departure time leave me with excessive leisure which, no doubt, a better man than I would spend in contemplation of eternal verities. Perhaps Allah, who does not deduct from a man's life-span the hours spent in hunting, might extend this dispensation to fathers held in suspended animation by the gentler sex's limitless capacity for second thoughts. Audible warning of it steals upon the ear.

'Who's not got a clean handkerchief? Well, go and get one then!' 'Gosh, I've let my watch behind' (she seldom consults it). 'I think

I need a warmer headscarf.' 'Who didn't turn the light off in the porch?' and then when all else fails, the heart-rending cry, 'I haven't fed my guinea-pig'.

The problem arises of how to pass the leaden-footed minutes. One can, of course, sit red-necked with rising gorge, drumming finger tips on steering wheel, with blood pressure mounting faster than the oil dial, stabbing the accelerator by way of hint. This achieves nothing, except damage to health, temper, and unit morale. Such demonstrations will cut no ice with *them*, clear-headed and ruthless as all women are from the cradle to the grave. They know what they want, and they will have it. They also know, of course, that I have fixed journey time to allow for dwelling a little at the start; or that if I have not, I should have.

Experience teaches me when to fear the worst. If the journey is a consequential one, as when setting off for Scotland, almost anything can be left behind with an easy mind. Who cares about tooth-brushes, pyjamas, even suitcases at a time like that? But lunch with friends, or church, are different. On each the toll of missing components, all strangely essential, falls like autumn leaves on Vallombrosa.

So, if wet, I sit and ponder. A man would have put his collection money in his pocket. Will the vicar be as gloomy as usual? Will Archie still be showing off his electric carving-knife? There was garlic in that paté last time. Thoughts come and go in the idle mind, for Nature abhors a vacuum.

If dry, a little exercise can be taken; or something attempted; something done. As a change from pacing the drive and clicking the gate-latch by way of encouragement, I once pulled forty groundsels from a rose-bed. The conservatory windows are seldom more meticulously adjusted than before a family exodus.

Sometimes, as in all life's more trying moments, there are unexpected rewards. On one grey day, as I lifted my eyes, perhaps in supplication, to a sky full of broken clouds flying over with a westerly at their heels, a sword-and-scimitar shape came swinging through them. I had seen flesh and blood fly so fast only over desert mountains and I knew that I was looking at a lanner. Off course? Lost by a falconer? How had it reached wet, soft Atlantic Britain from its harsh and arid homeland? The speculations flowed, but answer there was none. Instead the air was graced by cheerful, eager soprano voices. 'Come on,' they trilled, 'we're waiting.'

FEBRUARY 1977

FROZEN ASSETS

UPENDED LIKE A pair of dabbling mallard, we peered down into the arctic strata. Occasionally my wife decrees a reconnaissance in depth of the deep-freeze. This was one of the occasions, hence our semi-inverted posture. My rôle, as usual, was that of basket shifter and hoister-up.

Six baskets are arranged in banks of two. Below them is a further zone, of sub-glacial frigidity. To this the more senior contents sink when displaced by cross-postings to suit the kitchen's needs. Guests for Easter, and a subsequent lunch party, had impelled inspection of the bilges to assess what remained. Plenty did. Some of it had evidently passed temporarily out of the public eye some months earlier. The task of the basket shifter leaves small leisure and less breath for comment. Instead I made mental notes of some social consequences of the deep-freeze. As a universal below-stairs centre of influence it has replaced butler and cook in domestic economy.

Clean, snatch and jerk, and out came two baskets. Thus we had opened a passage between the frost-encrusted walls. Self-operated lights shone on goodies long immobilized, like treasures in the Hall of the Mountain King. Heave and shunt, and the frontage was extended. Labels testified not merely to the contents of packages, but also to some of my past life.

In its winding sheet of plastic foil lay a linear object. 'Trout, Itchen. 29/6/74', the legend read. Memory flooded back. The spring balance had said 3½lb. There was a time when I had daily expected to meet it again, decently clad in mayonnaise, the pink of it offset by the greenery of salad. Then, apparently, it had dropped out of the betting and into obscurity. Together we looked anew upon it. I said, predictably: 'Alas, poor Yorick.' She said, predictably: 'Crumbs, I'd forgotten that,' adding: 'Never mind, we'll mousse it.' It will be delicious. But whoever enjoys it will be denied the chance of musing upon the extent and symmetry of the trout's proportions, and of asking where, when, how and by whom it was caught. And I shall be denied the chance of answering.

'Let's have this out,' came in a change-of-subject tone. 'This' proved to be a plastic bag. The contents clanked ghostily and weighed enough to test the muscles of Precious Mackenzie. They comprised several components of the dismantled skeleton of a bullock. Soup of the evening has been more beautiful since their rediscovery.

Standing in Wessex, I plunged my arms repeatedly into Siberia. Two small knobbly objects proved to be a brace of grouse. 'They should be about right soon,' I remarked, trying to keep the one-upmanship out of my voice. I had seen the 1973 on the label. Some larger, more knobbly objects resembling chunks of basalt but showing brownish through the rime, were identified as casseroled chickens of more recent date, complete with trimmings. All that was necessary was to warm them up, and there was a ready-cooked meal. Very useful for emergencies. To prove it, we ate one for lunch. With a shock I descried the unexpended portion of last season's shooting. Pheasants by the dozen had been arrested at the crucial moment in the maturing process. Did I really bring so many home? Now they represented much of the protein element for the coming months. No less than the receiver of stolen goods, the deep-freeze motivates crime. The days during which, in unrevised legislation of the icehouse era of last century, possession of game was deemed innocent had elapsed. Even at that moment, technically speaking, we stood in danger of the judgment. That this should seem to a law-abiding household natural and not improper is one of the social consequences of deep-freezing.

We remembered feeling differently when, in our first deep-freezing year, we had served pheasant in July. This reckless act was perpetrated on a day when the Chief Constable dignified our table. The significance of his presence dawned too late for the menu to be revised. We watched him closely in case he choked, or reached for his notebook. He did neither. If, as seems likely, the long agenda of pheasant-eating is not completed by next July, we shall think nothing of offering it again, Chief Constable or no. Such is the permissive society.

More regrettable, to me, is the impetus which the deep-freeze has given to the acquisitive society. When, in pre-freezing days, I brought home a salmon the cry went out, Rejoice with us, and cuts were presented hither and yon. They still are, but fewer. That chaste white double cube, with its insatiable storage space, absorbs more for our own enjoyment than formerly we would have retained. The same applies to pheasants. Of those which will now dot our diet through the summer almost until their collateral descendants make their entry, about half would once have been given away. If the beef and mutton which, because of their availability, we shall not eat would as a result be deflected to somebody somewhere in need of food (and there are many such) my mind would be easier.

But this will not happen. Our deep-freeze, and everybody else's, is merely a fractional manifestation of the European beef mountain, an inevitable product of the age we live in and doing nobody any good. To share as neighbours becomes more difficult; self-provision becomes more necessary. At last the baskets were put back, sorted and reorganized. We ceased upending like mallard and again stood straight. The heavy white lid went down on, among other things, the simple pleasure of giving.

APRIL 1975

MICE AND MEN

NIP IN THE air at night has sent the mice indoors. Outposts of our house show evidence of infiltration. Now is the time to frustrate their knavish tricks, if necessary by slaying the little devils. The prospect brings no pleasure. To regard as enemies beneath one's roof such visitors as are unquestionably present in force beneath mine is uncomfortable for one whose relations with wildlife continue to be friendly. To trap seekers for shelter is the negation of hospitality, even if the necessity be undeniable. Additionally, I like mice.

By their tawny fronts and grey stomachs I deduce that ours are field mice, not house mice. Their readiness to move outdoors again in spring confirms this. They have clean glossy beauty. They also have the characteristics of mice the world over. The first is that although they have much to gain by keeping quiet they are quite incredibly noisy. One would not believe creatures so small capable of being heavy-footed. But they are.

Here in my dressing-room, at the end of the corridor far from the madding crowd, silence generally reigns. Not now. Using some secret track inside the walls, probably as old as any right of way in the village, mice have reoccupied the space above the ceiling. There they will stay through the hard weather months. And there, now, they are keeping themselves sound in mind and limbs. Apparently they play some mouse-version of Rugby football.

The rumble of their hoofbeats overhead as they form rucks and breakaways resembles a stampede of bison in a Wild West film. The sheer cheek and confidence of their behaviour amazes me. One would expect creatures reputedly furtive to conceal rather than advertise exercise of squatter's rights. They have, of course, weighed me up accurately. Slow to wrath (and somewhat idle), I shall take no action unless they commit a hostile act. This they have never done in eight winters as my neighbours. One came near it when I saw him shinning up the canvas case of a trout rod. But he seemed to know where he was going, and I wished him well. Had any lady of the household been present, a breach of the peace would have occurred. Another characteristic of mice is the hostility they evoke from womankind.

The distaff side, except when juvenile, have no sympathy for the wee cowerin' sleekit timorous beasties of Robert Burns. They see only the incarnation of all that is unnerving and evil. Even to suspect a mouse is for them to demand counter-measures. Already this autumn one mouse has attracted adverse publicity. My wife found it when she went to bed. It was couched on her electric blanket and was, moreover, reluctant to leave. Small blame to it on a chilly night. My suggestion that there was room for both of them received a dusty answer. Its appearance extended the zone of potential hostilities.

This permanently includes the apartment known, grandiloquently, as the boot hall. There footwear is changed, pony feeds prepared, and the door left open. To hear some recent situation reports, one might think mice had been marching in by column of threes. Outraged looks accompany these announcements and awaken that irrational sense of personal responsibility which is the burden all husbands bear.

So, since a man's first duty is to defend his family against the malevolence of the brute creation, out come the traps. The annual battle of wits, humiliating if I lose and disagreeable if I win, begins again. My plans are second nature now. Another characteristic of mice is that, clan by clan and generation after generation, they always do the same thing. The boot hall mice are heading for a warm corner near the boiler room. There they may eat stored tulip bulbs, search the pockets of my oldest shooting jacket for bits of dog biscuit, and drink condensation off an outflow pipe.

Not for long. One by one the traps will catch them. The season's bag will be about 30. It always is. I am not amused. My wish is that all the mice would be my guests and live in peace in that space above the ceiling over my head as I write. Mice have never done harm there, and the addition of another 120 pounding feet could not greatly alter the stupendous bedlam which the present occupants are already creating.

OCTOBER 1973

STRANGE INTERLUDE

AT ANY MOMENT now, we remarked with the wisdom of experience, we shall have total darkness. I found a torch, tested the battery, and put it handy. Lights blinked, and blinked again; the wind roared, and gutters gurgled. No country-dweller could doubt that electricity was about to fail. Somewhere a blown tree had fallen on a power line, or water invaded a transformer. Oilskinned men would have to seek the fault in the blackness of the night and amid the wildness of the weather. In such conditions, rectification would take hours. We awaited the inevitable. When it came, the silence was as complete as the darkness, and more noticeable.

Boon as it is, electricity inflicts a multiplicity of background noises. Being permanent, they eventually go unheard. When they stop, their absence is more evident than their presence ever was. So it was silence that epitomised the suspension of normality. No clocks ticked; all are electric. Suddenly I could hear my watch. From a distant bathroom the shrill complaint 'How the hell can I find my towel?' told that the world as a whole had not switched off. A sisterly response of 'Use your brains' confirmed that some normality remained.

However, action was needed, especially for those marooned upstairs. For such emergencies three oil lamps and a hurricane lamp are kept fuelled in the boot hall. Without noises-off the journey thither was through territory suddenly strange.

A modern kitchen can be vibrant and sonorous, even when potato-peeler, liquidiser and mixer have ceased work. But now its stillness was as macabre as the shadows thrown by the torch beam. The refrigerator hummed no longer. Even in neutral, the washing machine always seems to murmur, but now did not. The strip light, which generally buzzes half-heartedly as if it entrapped an anaemic wasp, was soundless, too. I felt an interloper there. The feeling intensified on opening the door beyond. The voice of the deep-freeze, its private gurgling a perpetual reminder of devotion to duty, was stilled with all else. None of the familiar gradations from idling to full blast came from the central heating boiler. Unnerved by the unfamiliar sound levels, our dogs barked at me.

Returning with my load of luminance, I found life as it had been, long ago. Our house contained ourselves alone. Alien presences neither beamed nor scowled from the window of the box. We were not being wooed, adjured, threatened or, worst of all, entertained. No guessing game was in progress. The contrast was not between life as it was, and as it had been before the power failure, but with life as it used to be when electrification was in comparative infancy. No voices except our own were to be heard, anyway for the time being. We asked each other what to do next. At other times the question does not arise; if a hiatus arises, one switches on the mesmerism, switching off all else.

The prospect was suddenly pleasurable. We were actually going to choose what was to happen, consulting each other and our own wishes instead of the *Radio Times*. In that calm freedom a Brahms symphony first seemed indicated, until realization returned that the record player is electric, too.

An hour passed, a rare valuable hour in which much was exchanged, from profundities to gossip. 'It's a long cut,' my wife remarked. 'We shall hear no news,' I said, as if it mattered. 'Why not?' came the response. 'There are two transistors in the house.'

So another vanished grace of living joined us. The radio, that now far off, comfortable companion of family evenings long ago, has dropped out of modern living. I had not thought of transitors as radio, relating them only to cricket scores in awkward places and pop music for those who enjoy it. But now, through a transistor, radio came back.

It was an improvement on the hectoring or simpering presence of television. It was a pleasure not to see the shabby cadaverous bearded men who in the late evening propound theories of vast inconsequentiality; another pleasure to be able to form one's own opinion of what was being described, instead of being limited to a miniaturised pictorial version. Especially when Hornblower came on the air. Even the oil lamps seemed intrusive then. C. S. Forester's words, and the scenes which grew from them, equated for the time being with the other near-lost pleasure of reading alone in total silence. He would have been a dull fellow who did not hear in them not merely what was said, but wind in rigging and tumbling sea.

Sometime in the small hours, electricity returned. Meanwhile, we had turned in. The bath water had been tolerable, and even with all radiators dead the house had not much chilled off. For living comfortably, we are duly grateful. But two hours with the date turned back to the dear departed 1930s was proof that not all progress is improvement.

APRIL 1980

UNDER THE SKIN

THINGS REMEMBERED SEEM superior to similar things experienced, perhaps because of the selectivity of memory which is one of life's mercies. That which was enjoyable may also prove unforgettable. Time discards the unremarkable and the unpleasant from the recollection system.

On the evidence of memory, and with rare and beautiful exceptions, the honest English sausage is a thing of the past, having been overwhelmed by internationalisation which has inflicted upon our proud people the relative insipidities of the Rhine Valley and the Lombardy Plain. Even in those reputed hotbeds of sausage design and manufacture, what an Englishman hopes for in texture, and will survive in flavouring, are evidently not understood. But the mass habit of holiday travel has led to their recipes being adopted in supermarkets here. The wurst and polony of the EEC have become acceptable to the customers, who have inflicted them upon their menfolk. They, conditioned by the declining standards in the quality of life, have in general regarded them as additional examples of blight and worsenment; unasked-for and pointless, but unavoidable, like decimal currency and altered county boundaries.

In general, but not in total. Here and there, amid the uniformity, guardians of the old art still produce sausages with the flavour of the 1930s. The hope of a return to such pleasures kept a generation at war masticating soya link through many a campaign. Some connoisseurs, myself included, know where to find them still, but we are few.

My personal source is an inn on a high road in Hertfordshire, which offers sausages specially made by a local butcher. I do not pass it without partaking of these lynch-pins of their luncheon trade. Afterwards the landlord wraps as many as he can spare to be put into the car and carried home to Wessex. Not that Wessex is devoid of old English sausages. Rumours are heard of a butcher on the verge of Salisbury Plain who retains the secrets of the art. Some may ask the nature of such secrets, and the characteristics which distinguish these surviving English sausages of the Imperial epoch.

First, they are pork sausages. Beef sausages are not relevant to this appraisal. Secondly, they contain no garlic, although onion in moderation is basic. They may be assessed by taste, aroma and visual inspection. The novice can most easily apply the latter. If the sausage meat is of the proper basic components and texture, and is inserted at the correct pressure, the skin will burst under frying. The result will be a slit along the convex side, with the fringe benefit of making the contents more accessible. The relish and nose of a good sausage depend largely on the herbal content. This is the aspect of sausage-making to which scant attention is paid on the European mainland with results as disastrous as the vapid Frankfurter. No master sausage maker reveals materials and methods, for obvious reasons, but personal analysis enables me to write with some authority.

Apart from onion, the main fortification of an English pork sausage is sage, with its invariable counterpoise, thyme. Marjoram and cloves, in subtle dispensations, exert their background effect. Some makers add mace, if only because mace can be added to anything without perceptible effect. For red-blooded customers pepper steps up the zest.

There, in some cases, the recipe stops. But not at my Hertfordshire inn. No sausage is held fit for consumption at the bar of that house without seasoning with ginger, lemon and nutmeg. The result is a delicacy, and a sustenance far transcending any mass production, alive with the fragrances of country England. It is something more, being a matter of pride produced by somebody with a joy in creating good things carefully. It is a joy which much of our population have largely lost, thanks to confusion between efficiency and cheapness.

AUGUST 1978

A TREE TOO FEW

TO SEE THE last of an elder tree is generally a pleasure. So, when my neighbour proposed the felling of one in which we had mutual interest, I agreed. And agreed without realizing what was involved. Senior elder trees should not be taken lightly. They have a way of making their presence felt, and their absence too.

This one grew on his land. So technically he need not have consulted me. But he did. Perhaps he had more than one motive. Courtesy was certainly one. He sensed, more clearly than I, that though he could well do without the tree, it had been conferring advantages on me. That I undervalued them was my own fault. Another impulse might have been an unconscious wish to share the decision. Elder trees have not lost their significance in the countryside. Traditionally they connote knowledge and wisdom.

Commonly they were grown outside the houses of witches, who were the herbalists of their day.

The spirit of the elder, subtle, powerful, benevolent but capricious, lives on in the back of our minds; anyway in mine, and by that token perhaps in his. To us the elder is the tree of the knowledge of good and evil. He might not wish to pronounce a unilateral death sentence if another would bear part responsibility. Of course our decision was not hurried. Several weeks passed between 'How would you feel if I had that old elder down?' and 'What about it then, that old elder we talked about? Thought any more, have you?'

This elder tree grew at his field gate at the south-western extremity of my ground, between me and the wind. He wanted new gate posts where he could not put them if the tree remained. In its lee stood our timber barn, used for storing hay and straw. I turned the meteorodynamics over in my mind, but other things counted more.

How long it had stood there could only be guessed. There had once been a cottage where the barn now stood, so the oldsters say. There was talk of a wise woman having lived there. Even in the nineteenth century a wise woman (a term of respectful fear, but not of love) would have qualified for the elder. Perhaps Nature should be allowed to end what she began. And there was no denying the tree's personal magnetism. Untidy and scrofular though she was in winter, wind-harassed and sodden from storms, she could and did dress well in summer. Her blossom, heaped like cream upon her, lasted weeks, making the tree a landmark for all who dropped down to the village from the surrounding hills.

My wife cut its flowers to make elderflower champagne. It produced more mildew than any other elderflower champagne has ever done, causing the faint-hearted to opt for nettle beer on hot summer nights. The mildew did me no harm. I took it as just a jocular spell laid posthumously by the wise woman on the heirs and successors of those who pulled her cottage down and built the barn instead. Certainly it was an elder tree of character.

But two grown men should be able to decide the fate of an elder tree, and together we did so. I was fortified by my dislike of elder in general. It intrudes, and will not go away. It puts curses on useful plants, so that they do not thrive in its vicinity. Thus the elder tree came down, and great was the fall thereof; a crack, a sigh, a crash, a great emptiness, and unexpected sky. Our senior daughter burst into tears, as she always does when a tree comes down, and I do not blame her. To dislike elder in general is one thing; not to mourn a tree in particular is impossible. When she learned that I had connived in the decision she gazed balefully and steadily at me, and I realized the fineness of the distinction (if it then existed) between man and brute. It took her half an evening to cheer up.

All that was twelve eventful months ago. The newly opened sky has lost its surprise factor. The mortal remains of that which had hidden it went up in smoke on Guy Fawkes night. But the elder tree lives on unseen, playing a greater part in our lives than ever it did in its days of visibility. In Nature nothing ends. Only form changes. In the close-knit interdependence of any small zone of life and weather, absence is as potent as presence. The elder tree does not let us forget.

The first gale after its demise stove in the gable end of the timber barn, when the wind's fist hit it with its guard for ever dropped. A new and malevolent air current, sweeping past the stables, flattened a pergola and has wrenched a ceanothus off its axis, leaving it bowed and cowering. On wet, dark nights when I do the last rounds, a concentrated douche of rain is shot at me from where the elder stood. When it scores a bulls-eye my cap vanishes until next morning, and I come in with soaking collar. And later, when a storm stacks up, its blasts are funnelled through the gap by the timber barn, and rise to a shriek, a cackling shriek, which we did not hear before.

The wise woman seems much amused.

October 1976

Friends and Neighbours

Through the essays runs the constant strand of Proteus's companionship with all the life around him. Whether wild life or human, this is unforced and amounts to simple acceptance. He does not sentimentalize, he merely welcomes. He suggests neither pressure group nor astringency, and is seemingly apolitical. But he still demonstrates the most British of paradoxes, that he to whom a dog is a dog and a cat a cat in the most plainly non-anthropomorphic terms, can still extend to them and receive in return an affection in no way lessened by understatement.

A LADY OF SENIORITY

EXCEPT FOR THE children asleep upstairs, the evening of a great storm found me alone in the house. My wife was attending that *sine qua non* of village life, a performance of *Blithe Spirit* in the Reading Room. Darkness had fallen and nobody else remained. I drank a little whisky and considered the next move. Would it be preferable to regale myself with Beethoven or Mozart? Or neither, but to listen instead to the wilder music of the wind as it eddied in the chimney and set the television aerial thrumming? In the event the record-player stayed silent. A new and mesmeric presence intervened.

Sitting on the arm of my chair, I realized, was the senior terrier. Her eyes were directed towards my face. It is three years since she saw me. Rising 10, she became suddenly and finally blind; and, being a fox terrier with all her lineage of courage and self-sufficiency, carried on much as usual. After nearly 13 years together we have small need nowadays of formal communication. We meet briefly at 7 a.m. when, after ceremonial yawning and stretching of stiffening limbs, she takes her first airing before Reveille sounds for the younger and more hobbledehoy gundogs. We seldom meet again until, all others having retired to bed or bath, I sit with a nightcap and think the thoughts that come with the ending of the day.

The senior terrier sits on the arm of the chair to think them with me. Tonight she was paying an unscheduled visit. She well knew that the evening was young because the junior terrier, not yet harboured in the kitchen, still slept post-prandially on the rug. Broken routine made the occasion special. Ears cocked, she held the salute with her sightless eyes. I returned her gaze, then stroked her neck. That she did not move represented an eloquent speech. She is a fastidious person and, though friendly to authorized strangers, disdains their touch. Neither will she encourage mine if there is an eye-witness to the familiarity. By remaining, she made this a telepathic moment. So we shared thoughts soundless, as one can with very old friends.

Her face, once bright tan with a blaze, is whitened now. The grey slash from eye to muzzle, left by a fox in her active-service days, has become invisible, merging with the sign of advancing years, just as the incident itself has been cut down to size by the other happenings of a long, full life. Old lady, I thought, you are nearer the end than the beginning. And realization came late that the same applied to me. Inevitably my mind turned to the business of growing old gracefully, untroubling to others. When the time comes, I hope I manage it as well as she does. In particular, I hope I shall be as meticulous as she is at keeping friendships green, and at evolving a design for living to fit declining powers.

She does not take much exercise nowadays. She even gave up the summer evening's stroll along the chalk track between the barley fields when asked to share it with a spaniel who, though well-meaning, had loutish manners. But she has no prejudice against youth in general. She chaperones the junior terrier with dignity, and is treated in response with the respect both given and taken by members of their patrician breed. She is in full possession of her faculties, as newspapers say of centenarians. Three rats learned this in the exodus at harvest. They will learn nothing else. What we haven't got, we'll do without is good terrier philosophy, and the senior terrier demonstrates that if you cannot see them you can still catch them. Sometimes a turning ear and a growl indicate that she had heard a cat stamping its feet on the lawn; nobody else can.

She is teaching her successor to adopt a superior air towards the gundogs. This old-fashioned social barrier fits her generation. The gundogs are working class. Terriers are members of the household. Not only the fact but the spirit of this distinction must be maintained, and will be while there is breath in her body.

Perhaps this will not be for very long. We have shared much together, times of ecstasy and desolation, but chiefly of bright contentment. She has cheered me by some of her triumphs and adventures, and I have wished I could have done something to inspire her in return. We have dug and hunted together, I have known the pleasures of her children, and she has given her heart to mine. When we part she will leave me incomplete, but richer for her comradeship.

One can think too much of the future.

September 1973

FACE AT THE WINDOW

LIFE IS POORER for lack of a cat. Our household must do without one. The senior terrier disapproves, and when the time comes for the junior terrier to reign in her stead it would be rash to expect a more liberal outlook. Even a cat prepared to spend an elevated existence on the tops of bookcases and the backs of the taller chairs would attract adverse comment. Harmony, in short, could not prevail. Hence a defelinized family in which memories fill the gap.

Before the senior terrier's time, indeed in a drab period of totally terrierless existence, a kitten had reported for duty. This is characteristic of cats. It is not necessary to seek them by prolonged study of advertisements, nor to buy them after haggling over the price. In their independent way they take matters into their own paws and make the decisions. If a vacancy exists, a cat fills it.

She was a mixture of smoke-grey and white, like a merle collie. She was prepared to do all the usual things for which kittens are renowned, such as playing with balls and pouncing on toecaps. But this was a case of 'on with the motley'. She knew she was expected to entertain and, out of the innate courtesy of all cats, she did so. But at heart she was a person of some gravity, and had a turn of mind both reflective and observant. She preferred to detach herself from the mainstream of life, and watch events flow quietly past. We were fellow spirits, and from this fact grew a relationship valuable to us both, and largely clandestine.

We did not, as a matter of principle, communicate until she indicated a readiness to do so. It seemed a proper basis for acquaintance with a lady. Less proper, perhaps, was her refusal to grant me an audience in daylight, or in the presence of a chaperone. She was solitary, a creature of the night, and her night included me. Not that she forgot me by day. She always seemed to know my whereabouts, although hers were shrouded in mystery. My return home never passed unnoticed. Always my eye would fall, somewhere between the garage and the door, on a composed figure with tail erect, walking in dignity along a path between the borders, almost invariably away from me.

To speak was unnecessary. The message had been delivered.

My return had been noted, and she had not failed to salute it. All else could be left until later. Later generally meant the hour before midnight. My study was downstairs, the curtains undrawn, the window a black square in winter; black until the familiar figure materialized on the outer sill. A ritual tapping on the glass with a soundless forefoot followed, with a soundless opening and closing of the mouth. Lip-reading interpreted 'I want to come in.'

So, night after night, she sat on the writing table. She watched the moving point of my pen. Sometimes she laid a gentle paw on the top of it. If, so doing, she prevented indiscretion she has my thanks; if she frustrated phrases golden enough to make me famous, I forgive her. No other moving, sensate being could intrude on my writing without breaking the spell of insulation and concentration. She became partner as well as spectator. Our companionship left pride, privacy and independence unimpaired for both of us. It was a relationship which added a little to one's understanding of the world and the people in it, be they human or not.

When the time came to leave that house it seemed wrong that she should leave too. Cats give something of themselves, but not all. They orientate on places, not on people as dogs do. The mint on which she had curled in the sunshine, the warm stone walls, the long grass where she had stalked, the trees where she had sharpened her claws all made her little world. My upheaval was not for her. The gardener inherited her. Years later, in passing, I called on the old man, and saw her again. She did not lift her head at my voice, but it was daytime so I did not feel she had cut me. She sat on the old man's knee. She never sat on mine. But he was arthritic and enjoyed the warmth.

FEBRUARY 1973

THE WRECKERS

WHILE STANDING EASY from morning fatigues at the salad frames I mused upon the moral turpitude of birds. To be reminded of its extent is a minor sorrow. I am one who believes that birds can do no wrong, until it is forced upon my notice that the contrary is true. And there, before my very eyes, was one culprit *in flagrante delicto*. A blackbird was hopping along a row of newly-planted onion setts. He gobbled a worm. Then he pecked out two or three more invisible goodies, to which he was welcome. But between times his eye would light upon the protruding top of a sett which he would then tweak expertly out of the ground, flick a foot or so to one side and leave lying. This conduct went well beyond a joke.

More than enough that I should need to walk the rows again in human hairpin posture, gathering and replacing the setts. What drove the iron deep into my soul was the identity of the guilty party. Hitherto I had assumed voles responsible. Such tiresome behaviour by them could be dismissed with the thought that it is their nature so to do. But that a blackbird, that peerless songster, should duplicate the mindless vandalism of a football supporter came as bitter disillusion. Of course I know blackbirds have their weaknesses; what *virtuosi* have none? But they are mainly those of jolly self-indulgence, such as the scrumping of strawberries, which can be frustrated by netting. Wilful damage to no purpose is another matter.

Considering that I produce cherries by the tree-load, from which the blackbirds benefit far more than my household, their attitude to onion setts is unethical to say the least, and their ingratitude sharper than a serpent's tooth. Yet nothing can be done about it except to repair the havoc and be thankful for the melody at noonday.

This philosophical conclusion was shattered by the sight of the first swallow. He sat on the stable power-line, adjusting feathers which his journey from Africa had left in disarray. While waiting for the others to turn up, he gazed with apparent approval at our home acre. He would have been able to note that little had changed since he left it last autumn. The iron went smartly back into my soul. Too right that little had changed. Soon his eye would stray towards the erstwhile cart shelter. Beneath its raftered roof our cars are parked, swallows nest and, worse, roost. Little doubt that all would be back to normal once he and his gang reclaimed possession.

If only they could contain themselves for just five more yards on flying out; or use a modicum of consideration for their hosts when deciding where to sit out the night; or employ a little self-control during its few brief hours. Small hope indeed. Henceforth each vehicle must be protected from unsightly and malodorous encrustation at the start of each new day. So they must be sheeted like racehorses when they are put away at night. At morning, taking off and folding the sheets will be an extra time-consuming task. Swallows make a summer. Sad that they should also make a mess.

A woodpigeon planed in and sat on a clothes post. He was of gross and corpulent aspect. And I knew why. He was stuffed almost spherical with the broccoli shoots which should have graced our table. W have enjoyed this delicacy once a week. But for the woodpigeon's depredations it would have been twice.

A robin flitted past. He must be watched. Last year he, or one of his kin, nested among the coils of 30 yards of hosepipe. That his little family should be disturbed in the interests of mere irrigation was unthinkable. We waited 10 days longer than usual for our first broad beans.

Some lights still remained to be lifted. It was time to return to the task. Bending my now rested back, I heard a screeching and a fluttering. Half a dozen excited sparrows, intent on some unknown ploy, went pell-mell past me in the general direction of the raspberries. Their urgency was no concern of mine. Sparrows, a noisy, vulgar, ill-mannered set, are the hooligans of yard and garden. But they win my heart on two counts. They are always cheerful. And despite their lack of polish, public relations and charisma, I have never known them to do actual harm, unlike some others higher in the social scale.

MAY 1974

UNDERGROUND MOVEMENT

MY MOLE IS now named Garryowen. Up and under is his favourite tactic. No Rugby player employs it more devastatingly. He ranks as mine although he has not been reduced into possession, as the lawyers say of *ferae naturae*. Clearly he regards himself as a vassal, his interests shared with me and entitled to exploit the resources of my soil. Furthermore, no other man of sound mind would volunteer to be his owner.

So for practical purposes, he is mine for keeps, or until he elects to quit. The contingency seems unlikely. He is impervious to hints. Were it possible to have an eyeball-to-eyeball confrontation between man and mole, we have been having one since February fill-dyke. The plot which he has made his manor is remote and secluded at the topmost salient of the kitchen garden, separated by only a hedge and an unfrequented path from downland where vetch and restharrow dot the lynchets. We overwintered parsnips there. Whenever I went to lift some, his night's heavings met the eye.

Neither moles nor anything else harm parsnips. When the crop is changed to brassicas the story differs. Now he erupts like a land mine below seedling after seedling, darkening my countenance with bile and spleen. One cannot reasonably expect him to go and erupt elsewhere. In this arid summer, he has chosen his ground realistically. Normally, one would not expect moles on a topmost salient in the warm months. Most of them move downhill, where the water is. Non-stop digging builds up a rare thirst, and moles are heavy drinkers.

This mole has become aware of trickle irrigation, and its effects. The waterlines keep each row of transplants cool and moist. Worms gather in the underlying strips. Scenting them in the subterranean darkness, the mole has no incentive to go elsewhere. So wherever he surfaces to throw out spoil, he is in reach of vulnerable plants. I cannot blame him. In his situation I hope I should have the intelligence to act similarly. But in defence of my proper enterprises, few courses are open. Perhaps I could trap him. This I have no wish to do while even a fading chance remains that he will voluntarily decide on new hunting grounds. Perhaps, if he hears they have had a better rearing season over the boundary, or that the worms are shown better there, he may decide to leave my syndicate.

Strychnine I neither use nor connive at. Several seasoned old countrymen have suggested deterrents, but the advice of seasoned old countrymen is best ignored by all except enthusiasts for wasting time. Co-existence seems inevitable.

Only once, so far, have the mole and I actually met. He surfaced near my boot when I had been standing stationary for five minutes or so (not wasting time, be it noted, but committing to memory the distinctive notes of missel and song thrush). The encounter might have been dramatic. It was as if Guy Fawkes had popped up in the Lobby of the House of Commons, face to face with Mr Speaker. Being British, the mole and I carried off the situation urbanely.

The pink of his nose amid the convulsing tilth provided an opportunity for a knock-out. I did not take it. One does not assault the blind. As for him, he dived back into Mother Earth with a speed and skill which showed me the life of the mole in a new light. Instead of the laborious sapping and mining of men when tunnelling, moles porpoise through the soil as if doing a butterly breast stroke, taking the quick and imperceptible breaths of swimmers. Decent, hard-working little fellows as they are, it is good to see them masters of their element.

Those whom we admire, we learn to tolerate, even if their activities be regrettable. Day by day the small round barrows continue to mark my mole's comings and goings. The foot stamping needed to counteract them, combined with the maledictions which then come so readily to mind, act as safety valves for stress in general. Moles may have their uses after all.

JULY 1975

UP IN SMOKE

FEW ENTERPRISES ARE more fraught, and if successful, more satisfying, than the ancient rite of burning off the rubbish. To set a match to that which is no longer wanted, and watch it go up in smoke, may seem a simple thing. Appearances deceive.

Complexities surround it. The occasion has its own terminology, even its own ethics. This being the bonfire season, they constitute a heavy but not unpleasurable load upon the mind. It is necessary first to define 'rubbish'. In this context the word has more precise application than its usual meaning of anything superfluous, noxious and disposable, including non-organic matter such as waste paper, worn-out car tyres and old tins. Rubbish, to us of the land, is essentially vegetation which has served its purpose or had no purpose at all, and is at least semi-combustible.

Nevertheless these limits cover so wide a field that the blending of the contents of a bonfire is not to be lightly undertaken. It can be achieved, having regard both to the objective and to the finer arts of attaining it, only by old hands. This category excludes women, beardless youths (the term may be metaphorical nowadays) and persons clueless in elementary botany. The objective is that the original pile of root and branch, however vast and rugged it may be, however many weeks its assemblage may have occupied, shall be converted in one uninterrupted process into pale grey residue, rich in potash, friable in texture, and free of unoxidised matter. He who brings this about may reflect upon his achievement with pride if, in doing so, he has fulfilled two conditions. They concern the safety and comfort of his neighbours.

First, it is a point of honour that a well-conducted bonfire exudes smoke but never flame. Those exhilarating, Stromboli-like performances, beloved of the young at such times of merry-making as Guy Fawkes night, are anathema to serious practitioners. Windborn sparks are hazards to thatched roofs and ricks. Moreover, such a blaze, easy-come and easy-go, produces ash of reduced quality and far from free of contents only semi-burned.

Secondly, the smoke must not offend others. Burning must happen only when the wind is set in a quarter which precludes this, and when there can be reasonable expectation of it staying there until it has dispersed the last faint whiffs. Since this may be a week later, contingencies must be foreseen. A bearing which on Saturday sees the occupants of a neighbouring cottage breathing easily may on Monday pose dire consequence to their washing line. Experience of operating an artillery board gives best chance of avoiding embarrassment.

So, for the weeks in which 'rubbish' has been piling up the best brains of the household (which in this instance happen to be mine, if only through temporary want of an alternative) have planned the manner of its piling. At times like these a hot bottom is much esteemed by countrymen. Lest the term confuse, it means swift and vigorous generation of heat in the central depths of the fire, sucking in air, circulating it, and drying the next layers to be consumed. For this the small, round, oily leaves of lonicera are ideal. So the pile is built up around barrow loads of clippings from the formal hedges. As it grows, the year's history repeats itself in detritus.

A tangle resembling an ancient field telephone is identified as runner bean haulm in time of corruption. An odious, blackened mass was once a flourish of dahlias. An unwelcome handful of thorns reawakens the fresh flavour of the summer's raspberries. Pitch up the wreckage. Who cares? There is another year ahead. And another bonfire. More weeks may pass before I judge the moment ripe to walk the windward side with a twist of burning straw. But when it comes, and if all goes well, to stand aside and watch what follows will be my pleasure.

Fire, man's elemental enemy, working as an ally in a manner pre-ordained is a sight always worth seeing. To watch any plan go right is a moment of mastery. One has a right to enjoy it, to reflect upon the contrived sequence of cause and effect, to be satisfied at achievement. Duties will remain, of course. At first and last light unburned material must be pulled around to close weak points where burning threatens to break into the outer air. Collapse of the inner structure will shrink the once-great pile. But come frost or downpour nothing stops a well-built, well-cared-for bonfire until its inner core glows more deeply red and dies into a week or so of neutral, pulsating, slowly-fading heat.

At such a moment, look around. The scene is barer than it was. We have made space for spring.

December 1974

CASUAL WATER

WHILE THERE IS breath in my body one patch of wetland will be safe from the draining which is having unhappy effect on birds and butterflies. This is the puddle outside our gates. Let none treat it with contempt. As a service to wildlife it probably achieves more than any bird-table. This claim will be substantiated anon. Its educational and entertainment values are both immense. And it is not without impact on human affairs.

To take the last-named first, the puddle is so situated as to cause let or hindrance to such as come and go. This includes me, though I have grown wise to it. Only five or six yards in diameter, expanding, contracting, and occasionally disappearing according to season, it has a knack of escaping the notice of others who arrive in cars. When a vehicle is positioned ready to enter, driver or passenger prepares to alight to open the gates. It is then that the puddle's rippling surface and glutinous surroundings are seen to await the human foot. The car must be reversed and the gate-opener decanted on to dry land.

Of course, when visitors are expected the gates are left ceremoniously wide. This does not absolve me from an accusation of failing to remove inconvenience to others. I plead mitigating circumstances. Forty yards away, and in full view from the dining-room window, what happens there is known to us. The boons which the puddle confers on other residents in the village, and visitors too, are at least some justification for its existence. If birds spoke, the votes of thanks would be many.

Martins come from far and wide for building material. To them the chalky mud from the edges must rank as, say, Carrara marble does to us. Sometimes a dozen are loading up simultaneously, a task which averages at about 15 seconds. Allowing two minutes to reach the nest, use the mud, hawk a fly or two, and return, and we must be providing material for 100 martins' nests. We seldom have more than four under our own eaves. No case has been reported of a village martin's nest coming unstuck. Ours must be mud of special adhesiveness. We shall continue to supply it. Swallows use it too. But their need for reliability in components is less as their nests do not hang, but are built on solid bases.

Without our puddle, problems would arise in maintaining avian hygiene. It is the public bath for, in particular, starlings, sparrows, blackbirds, thrushes. Enthusiasm for the tub seems to rank in that descending order. Starlings appear to enjoy ablutions most. They splash and sluice and jabber with uninterrupted energy. Sparrows are communal bathers, arriving in noisy gangs like the village boys rushing to the river pool after school on a hot day. Like village boys, they splash each other and start fights. Sadly, the thrushes and blackbirds are not only solitary bathers, but silent. It would be a pleasure if these accomplished melodists sang in the bath, as less accomplished humans do. I do recall a bar from either.

Other wings, more glorious than theirs, are seen on hot days. Butterflies, the *nymphalidae* especially, come for water or to seek putrefaction in the mud. I have seen peacocks, painted ladies, red admirals, tortoiseshells and commas open their beauty to the touch of the sun. Once a dragonfly, badly off course, inspected our puddle cursorily, but decided it was beneath his notice and best left to birds.

Sometimes we see a welcome stranger, or signs of a turning season. A bullfinch flashes his heraldic colours. Goldfinches and linnets, unseen in summer, will tell us that autumn has begun. The puddle has another use in the weeks to follow. It is a favourite drinking place. But in temperate weather there are alternatives. When frost seals these, I ascend in the scale of benefactors.

It is a simple thing to go to the gates each morning and put a boot heel through the ice on the puddle. The flutter which follows when my back is turned is eloquent of an urgent need. When a woodpigeon or stock dove is seen to join in, I am thereby warned. Both species are pure-water fanatics. They prefer to drink from cattle troughs which, being deep, give a draught free from disturbed sediment. Their acceptance of the puddle's cloudy vintage indicates that all troughs are frozen, and that I must walk the fields with a crowbar.

How our puddle comes to be where it is, and why it seldom dries out, only geologists could determine. I shall not ask them to do so. Such men eat of the tree of knowledge of good and evil, and would tell me how to drain it. I do not want to know.

JUNE 1974

Horse Senses

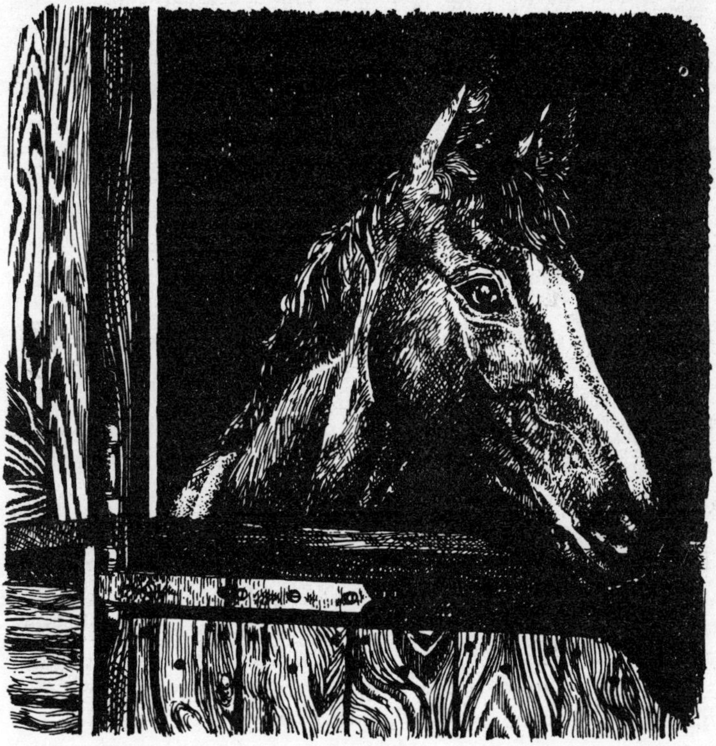

This is the golden age for horses. As employees they have become redundant, but in their new status in which they join dogs and cats as companions and court jesters to human households they continue to thrive. This subject race, their centuries of forced labour and exploitation behind them, now exist in an aura of privilege, significant only in our recreations on which the Proteus sidelight falls.

JUST HEARSAY

As HAS HAPPENED before, my wife bought a horse. This time she performed the ultimate in intrepidity by advertising her wish to do so in cold blood and cold print and inviting offers to our telephone number. We soon learned a thing or two.

She sought, said the advertisement, a confidential cob, not without a turn of foot, on which she could ride out with some prospect of keeping in touch with our daughters. It has been my experience that those who ask intelligent questions may receive silly answers, especially about horses. We did. It fell to my lot to take some of the calls.

I never became cad enough to hang up on hearing the doom-laden words, 'We've got just the one you're looking for.' But I learned what they meant. It seemed polite to let the speaker rabbit on a bit. Given time and some amiably pitched grunts into the hand-set, we would eventually reach the bit about the touch of navicular that had never bothered him, or the laminitis three years ago that she's never given a hint of since. Then negotiations could be broken off on an appropriately understanding note.

Not being wholly void of faith in human nature, I was aware that one in a hundred such claims might be genuine. I was also aware that the odds were three-to-one against it turning up in the first 25 responses. That was about the number of calls I took. Only one caller left me with a burning desire to shake his hand. That was the sepulchrally-voiced would-be vendor who opened with the illuminating statement, 'We wondered if perhaps you'd take this one off our hands.' We would not, but we admired integrity, if not acumen.

I faithfully made notes in every case and passed them to the level of decision. Signs appeared that something was cooking. 'Do we know of a vet near Exeter?' I was asked. We did not, but we knew who should. I telephoned a spritely young woman.

'A vet?' came the response in tones of soaring incredulity. 'What on earth for?' 'We want him to look at a horse.' 'A horse?' Incredulity was going through the upper register. 'I trust you know what it will set you back.' 'I can guess,' I said. 'Don't you ever use vets?' 'Only for dogs,' came the answer, 'I don't know much about dogs. Anyway, leave it to me.'

A vet reported. No deal. 'I bet she bought it herself, and buttoned her lips,' said my wife. I did not say anything. No man would, in those circumstances. That is one of the differences.

Time passed. Something else began cooking. One day my wife hitched up the trailer and drove away. Two hours later she was back. 'Stand clear,' she said as I lowered the tail-gate. Out popped a large and important-looking horse. Very large, even for summer. His lofty, charitable gaze gave him a noble look. 'Well, what do you think?' she asked. 'He's not very fit.'

To me he looked fit to burst at the seams. I walked round him, seeking grounds for comment which would be both valid and inconsequential, and gain me time. 'Feet need seeing to,' I ventured. 'Too right, I'll phone the farrier.'

Within a week the farrier arrived, with assistant, in their neat little van. 'Well, well, what have we here, then?' he inquired. His assistant stared in speechless concentration at the newcomer in the paddock. 'That the one?' he asked. We nodded.

'That's the sod that stunned the vicar,' declared the young man with heart-felt clarity. 'Did he come off of a parson's daughter?' This time I left my wife to do the nodding.

The farrier spoke in measured terms. 'He's the one that run up the hayrick,' he pronounced. 'You wasn't there when he stunned the vicar,' pursued his assistant. 'Served the old buzzard right, he'd no call to be standing there, doing no good.'

'And you wasn't there when he run up the hayrick,' countered the gaffer. But the time for reminiscence had passed. 'Well?' I asked.

The farrier made us proud to be British. He drew a deep breath. 'He's shoeable,' came the ruling. He was, but it was one of the Iron Duke's damned close-run things.

June 1978

VAIN THINGS

ONE TRANSACTION DOES not alter. It is the sale or, to put it more bodefully, the purchase of a horse. Mankind's astutest brains have borne upon the matter across the centuries. There is one near-certainty about it. This is that the buyer of a horse does not acquire what he pays for. Go to market and put down £400 for a bullock, and all present will agree that one gets £400 worth of bullock to within 50p either way, no more, no less, at the prices ruling in the place and on the day, precisely that. It is different with a horse.

Go to auction or do a deal to buy a horse for £500, or £2,000, or £40,000, and all present will agree on one thing only; the buyer needs his head seeing to. Dark and numerous will be the cautionary tales, once the bargain has been struck, of past history and future hazard. Hence the frequent recourse after such decisions to that prince of nerve tonics, whisky.

The raw-boned four-year-old which slimmed your wallet by £400 is worth almost anything, except £400. It throws two splints in a month, has to be turned out for six, and is roaring when taken in again. It takes a chap like a QC on the next rostrum to squeeze £150 for him. Or perhaps it reveals a pop like a grasshopper and you spend the next decade wondering why you let it go show-jumping for a mere £1,500.

The £2,000 six-year-old is not worth it either. Far from it. He wins three hunter-chases on the trot, almost literally, all by eight lengths or more and poses the agonizing question of whether to take the £15,000 to which an ace trainer will go, or wait for a better offer. Or perhaps he is duck-hearted, and becomes a patent-safety for £800.

As for the £40,000 yearling, we all know what happens to him. In his first two-year-old stakes he runs green and makes no show. In his second he hates the mud, and makes no show. In his third he cannot act on a left-handed course, and makes no show. In his fourth he just makes no show, and nobody any longer cares why. At £800 and added to the list he fades away, to reappear in a new name as a show hack three years later, having been resold twice for less each time. Or he wins a Classic and is syndicated at a quarter of a million.

These daunting thoughts invade my mind to recall the awesome possibilities which await those who buy horses. They loom the larger because, in a manner of speaking, I recently bought one. The purchase introduced measureless extra unknown quantities. It was a pony for the children. Beside a pony, even a horse is comparative simplicity. Whether a Classic candidate or a traffic-proven hack ('suit nervous lady in seventies'), the requirements are at least equine. It is different with a pony.

As every father knows, a pony for the children must have human and mechanical qualities too, including the benignity of an archdeacon, the paces of a ballerina, the prudence of a butler, the durability of a prop-forward and the adaptability though not the appearance of a lunar module. Such a paragon is difficult to find, to put it mildly. When found, after months of search and repeated disappointment, *pater familias* is apt to be something near a nervous wreck, the victim of every insecurity from wild surmise to rank suspicion.

The charming family with whom it has done time suddenly seem less real and more apparent. What if their social ease and general pleasantness are cloaks assumed to hide more sinister characteristics? Are they, perhaps, a wily and grasping clan, of deep financial acumen as well as histrionic talent, passing on pony after pony to their handsome profit? When a horse looks over the door, charity flies the yard gate.

Nevertheless, the moment comes when the two outwardly urbane heads of families assume the traditional attitudes of contestants in man's most testing duel of wits. The gimlet-look sharpens the eyes of the otherwise blandly assured vendor until even Genghis Khan would quail. The buyer flexes his muscles for that semi-turn of the shoulders in the direction of the car, timed to the split second, which interrupts the routine stuff about sending him back if you don't like him (just try it, with a family of daughters freezing the atmosphere, and well the seller knows it).

Finally, with a suddenness which is both relief and climax, the thing is done, all passion spent. What we gave for the pony is my affair. Now I am wondering what he is worth. Time will tell.

FEBRUARY 1973

HELPFUL WORDS

ANNUALLY A SKIP arrives in the village. It is a large, steel, orange-painted container about four feet deep and similar, except for colour, to a tank without its tracks. Into it households pitch a ton or two of scrap iron and refuse too heavy for normal collection. My wife's horse, a stout-hearted fellow who bats no eyelid at the school bus with its shouting occupants or the milk tanker with its hissing air brakes, has reservations about the skip. He is a high-blower, and on approaching it he snorts like a machine-gun, relapsing when past into eloquently heavy breathing for the next hundred yards.

Until last week I attributed this to distaste rather than to suspicion. A horse with a strong sense of what is seemly, and there are many such, cannot be expected to withhold comment from what is undoubtedly a temporary blot on the landscape, however beneficial its purpose. His snorts and suspirations echo the sentiments of some crusty old colonel, with whom he would have much in common.

'Bless my soul (snort). The damn' thing's there again (snort). Horrible shape. Ghastly colour. Why can't they hide it away? Place is not what it used to be.' Etc.

All that having been implied, he has hitherto passed it without loss of dignity by either of us. Until last week. He was then approaching the skip in his normal manner – head high, ears pricked, eyes focused in shocked disbelief, sidling past so as to keep it squarely in his field of vision – when a new element obtruded. Two lads of the village, aged about 12, had hidden in the skip. Hearing the sound of hooves, they chose that moment to stand up.

At horse's head level, the skip thus seemed to have grown two heads, before his very eyes. This was too much. There was a prompt explosion, and a period of instability ensued. When this was sorted out I turned again head on to the skip and asked the two heads if they had wanted to have me written off. They said they did not know. Inadequate as this response seemed to me, it entirely satisfied the horse.

Instantly, he calmed down. Relaxed in nerves and muscles, he surveyed a bit nearer as though to see if they had legs. Fear had vanished because they had spoken with the tongues of men, if not of angels.

In the machine age, non-horse people forget that horses are not machines also but share the apprehensions which afflict us all. In particular they do not like mysteries, or things going on behind their backs. Somebody should produce a code of action for use by those decent enough to have some regard for horses and the people on their backs, but not knowing what to do. Three situations occur regularly in which attempts to be helpful achieve the reverse effect.

The first is when an approaching pedestrian senses, no doubt from my careworn expression, that I am on a neurotic horse, and courteously stands still and silent for me to pass. This may well make passing impossible. A human figure apparently dead in an upright position does not calm a horse's fears. It becomes a source of disquieting speculations. Is it human after all? Or a ghost? Or a visitor from outer space? To be simultaneously mute and motionless seems unnatural.

'Please speak,' I say, in such circumstances.

'What do you want me to say?' is a general and reasonable reply.

'Nothing, now,' is the only possible answer as, with doubts removed by these seven monosyllabic words, the horse strides cheerfully past, leaving behind another neighbour questioning my sanity.

Motorists whose cars are stationary with the engines running, a normal form of conversation piece outside the shop, are often considerate enough to switch off. This is fine, so long as they pick a good moment for switching on again. After the horse has gone 10 yards is not one of them. While the engine hums, the horse knows where the car is; when it is silent the horse is kept in suspense. When the starter whirrs close behind a horse which is fearing the worst, a galvanic leap is not to be wondered at. That the rider knows this as well as anybody adds nothing to his or her peace of mind.

Car followers of hounds have a well-intentioned habit of stopping and switching off to give priority to a rider entering the road from a field. His horse may then he presented with the oblong shape of the car, visible through a leafless hedge. An experienced hunter will be too interested in the hunt to be bothered by this. Not so a green one. Fearsome possibilities invade its mind.

Straight lines are not part of Nature. An oblong object is therefore suspect. But if the engine is left running, the horse knows it is a car; if an occupant gets out and speaks, the horse recognises a human adjunct, as when the lads in the skip gave brief evidence of their species. If neither happens, it remains that unnerving thing, an unknown quantity.

May 1980

TIME FACTOR

THIRTY-FIVE PACES FROM the kitchen windows, the grey pony starts each day in contemplation of small events in the meadow beyond the stables. Rabbits feed. Blackbirds argue over boundaries. Pigeons drink at the trough. She misses nothing and small things interest her. These include my own movements, which culminate in the arrival of her feed bowl and hay before going out to pasture. As soon as I enter the kitchen to make early tea she shifts her gaze to me. Thereafter she monitors my movements from window to window until, blissful moment for her, I emerge into the open and qualify for my morning whinny. It is a pleasant little sequence. It would also be unremarkable had it not held for weeks the core of an unsolved mystery.

It was good to know that her owner's father is more important than rabbits, blackbirds and wood pigeons. But it was baffling that I should become so only on arrival at the working top on which the tray is placed with the stores required for the brew-up. The pony's surveillance of the meadow demands a line of sight directed away from the house. How, therefore, could she (her back turned towards me) know of my arrival at the spot where, if she should swing her head through nearly 180 degrees, our eyes would meet? The clue long eluded me. Drawing the curtains of my dressing room I found her invariably deep in thought, head over the box door, looking away from the house. On my way to the kitchen I checked at each window that she had not moved. No reason why she should, since the whole house was in her blind arc. Yet, as my hand reached for the tray, she never failed to turn her head my way.

Having eliminated sight as the communicating link, I then ruled out touch and taste as inapplicable. A week of checking the wind direction disposed of scent, though stranger things have happened. Only sound remained.

At first sound seemed as positively excluded as sight. I am not clumsy, and at that hour wear soft-soled slippers. There seemed no point at which she, or anybody else could hear me, even inside the house, let alone from outside. So, I took a leaf from her book and monitored my movements. The truth was simple. Not quite all the stores for the brew-up were placed on the tray. The kettle was not. The kettle is electric, sited just inside the kitchen door. Each day in passing, I had switched it on in a movement so automatic that it was no longer a conscious one. The faint clink thus made had been picked up by the pony 40 yards away, despite closed windows. In the time taken by me to cross the kitchen to the tray, her head had swung round and her eyes had focused on the pane behind which, experience taught her, she would see me.

Prosaic as its components are, this little chain of cause and effect had its lessons for me. It indicated the acuteness of that pony's hearing and her ability to recognize the significance of the sound among many others, and to relate it to her own affairs. How often are the other senses of the horse similarly underrated?

So light a touch, if precisely applied, will produce such response that one wonders at the delicacy of so large and athletic an animal. Its far gaze will follow the movement of hare and fox across fields half a mile away. I do not believe it possible to approach a horse unheard, which makes it important that one should never try. The horse sense of taste is uncanny, especially among the more pampered and epicurean thoroughbreds. Note the disapproval bestowed on a bit of patchy meadow hay. And a horse's nose is probably as good as a gundog's.

The pony in question well knows my habit of carrying a cube or two when I go to lead her in from grass. And I know her habit of quickly frisking my pockets to find them while I slip the halter on. But never when, by culpable negligence, they have been forgotten. Then the sentiment, 'What have I done to deserve this?' is conveyed more eloquently than would seem possible. A haughty aloofness on her part, and an apologetic mien of mine, characterizes our return to stables.

The truth is that in most ways the horse is a bad communicator. Because of this we conclude that its comprehensions, both by the physical senses and otherwise, are limited. So, indeed, they are, if the more varied perceptions of the dog be taken as a yardstick. But the longer I live the more clearly I see that they are less limited than we think.

May 1976

UNSEEN PRESENCE

NEEDLES ARE REPUTEDLY ELUSIVE in haystacks. Never having mislaid one in such surroundings, it is not for me to pronounce on the validity of this folklore. All I can say is that a bay horse in a six-acre field on a moonless night must be similarly difficult to find. Compared with a needle, a horse is a large object, unlikely to become invisible by slipping into a nook or cranny, and dissimilar from anything else the field is likely to contain. But it nevertheless cannot be seen. Anybody who doubts this is welcome to put the matter to test.

In turning out the horse at dusk I had acted in good faith. He always is turned out at dusk in winter, having a coat thick enough to withstand the weather in Siberia, where horses originated. Moreover the field contains numerous snug refuges among hawthorn clumps curtained by old man's beard, as cosy as any stable. That this was the one night in all the year when to turn him out would be inopportune became apparent only when his owner, to whom I am married, returned home. She had chauffered a daughter to the school's end-of-term charity disco, a horrendous occasion from which I had steered well clear. To have failed to turn the horse out would have seemed a dereliction of duty.

But surely I remembered her intention to put a saddle on him next day and ride him round the lanes for a few miles? It was all part of the plan for keeping his legs right. That was why she had spent a good hour after lunch getting the mud off him.

The mind works fast in crisis. Now was the time for action. Within seconds I had donned duffle coat, cap and gum boots, seized head rope, apples and torch, and was heading for the field. I had put down some hay to help him through the long dark hours. If I could get to him before he finished it, I might also get to him before he rolled. If not, then I bitterly thought of the morrow. Part of it would be spent with curry comb and dandy in hand. Decency would permit nothing less. Of course the hay was finished. A few fragments, none more than three inches long, showed where I had pulled out the flake. This fellow absorbs hay like a suction pump. The questions loomed, Where had he gone? And what was he up to? So long as I could engage his attention, he would not roll.

That I had engaged his attention as soon as I entered the field was speedily apparent. So was his initial determination to stay out of contact. The attractions of the hawthorn labyrinth outweighed the comforts of his box. This was where he expected to spend the night, in company perhaps with a passing fox, field mice, their enemy the barn owl, and far-away lapwings unseen but not unheard. The wet turf exhaled a vapour fresh in its touch on the skin, aromatic to the nose. Pleasant as it was, it was unwelcome. Its mistiness neutralised the torch beam, which consequently shone into nothing – 360 degrees of nothing which somewhere held a horse.

This was not in doubt. Squelching footsteps and occasional snufflings proclaimed his presence on various bearings in the encircling gloom. I spoke his name. The approach was dismissed with scorn. Once or twice I may have seen him when an irregular patch of darkness seemed to move ahead of me. At last I actually did see him, or part of him; one eye, to be precise, reflecting back the torch-light which it had caught, a strange disembodied orb higher above ground level than it should have been. It looked like being a slow catch. I switched off the torch lest the battery ran out, and began to stalk him slowly.

Soon I made contact with a hawthorn branch, which relieved me of my cap. Retrieving it took time. This reminded me of something a wiser man would not have forgotten. While I extricated tweed from thorns I realised that the horse had come nearer. Curiosity conquers all, especially with domestic animals. The tactic was to stand still, await my chance when he edged up to me, and then make contact. It sounds easy, but was not.

Eventually he was very near. The air was so full of horse that I convinced myself I felt his warmth. I shone the torch again, but still could not see him. His winter coat, rough and unreflecting, threw back no image. Then I heard him breathing, reached for the head collar, and found myself with a handful of tail. Luckily I knew my horse, and he knew his man; no risk of him letting one go. When I had held on long enough, and he had accepted the fact, I moved my free hand over his croup, along his back, and up his neck to fix the head rope.

No light was needed to answer the all-important question. I had felt no wet soil on his hair, no shreds of pawed-up grass, no pressurised sycamore leaves which are his normal adornments after floor exercises at his favourite place. All was well. He had not rolled. The scrumping sound of an appreciatively masticated apple accompanied us home.

DECEMBER 1979

FINE HERBS

ONLY THOSE WHO do not know animals regard conversation with them as mythical or impossible. Admittedly animals cannot articulate. But certainly they can communicate with those they choose for the privilege, and they take good care that we get the message.

My daughter's pony is an example. Being a gelding he has the status of an honorary male. He and I are the only non-feminine individuals in an establishment otherwise populated entirely by mares, bitches, does, whatever is the female of guinea-pig, and women. The fellow feeling characteristic of small minorities enables us to exchange thoughts. We have our reservations about the opposite sex. The pony is more successful in his dealing with them than I am. Notably this is the case with the lady rising eight who rides him. Having reduced her to a desirable humility by a graduated series of shocks and surprises, he then takes the greatest possible care of her. This should be the policy of every husband.

But he does not talk to her, as he does to me. Between us, words are unnecessary. A roll of an eyeball, a twitch of an ear, a snort, a narrowing of the nostril, a stamp of a hoof, a toss of the head, a swish of the tail can, singly or in combination, convey as much as syntax and prosody, and sometimes more. From him I learn great truths.

After Christmas, to save my legs on a crowded morning, I put him into the mini-paddock. He was there only for an airing but the grass offered enough to amuse him. With broom and rake I turned to clearing the gravel of debris from the night's storm, ready for lunch guests. Out of the tail of my eye I saw the pony regarding me with undisguised chill; and, significant detail, not eating. To hell with you, I thought, knowing his mind, and kept my back turned as long as possible. Eventually I relented, as he had known I would.

I walked over to the paddock rail. By now the pony had assumed the head-high, proud-but-resigned posture of offended nobility. 'What the devil's the matter with you?' I asked.

He lengthened his muzzle to the position of extreme pessimism, curled a lip to express distaste, indicated the sward, and declared: 'Hogwash. And hogwash, moreover, of a high order. I have not lived nearly six years to hazard my digestion and affront my taste buds with such revolting fill-belly. I am surprised that a man of your sensibilities should expect me to. Prejudiced and inflexible you frequently are, but boorish and devoid of a sense of *comme il faut* you have not previously been. Pray adjust the arrangements.'

Those aware that such statements can be conveyed from beast to man, and who therefore know ponies, hardly need telling what followed. Off we went down the lane, to the little close which has never known plough (and also to the detriment of the morning's time-table). Its grass seemed short enough for a bowling green. The pony began expertly to shave off yet another wafer-like layer. After the first mouthful, he pronounced it perfect. Not for the first time either. To get it is what his soul desires. He will not pass the gate.

Perhaps the reason lies in the words 'never known plough'. Nothing save the incidents of Nature has composed its long-matured turf. Man has eradicated nothing and added nothing. The soil, chalky but not poor, has collected the grasses and the herbs most suited to itself and blended them, probably for centuries, into its own balance of vegetable and mineral. The pony, bred to the frugalities of his ancestral Wales, knows what is good, and is unimpressed by the winter offerings of lush and scientifically composed pasture in the mini-paddock. The reason for this preference, familiar to all who know livestock, seldom strikes home.

Most of us know fields in which, for undefined reasons, horses show a summer bloom weeks earlier than elsewhere. A Scottish friend, renowned for his beef cattle, thanks God for a single field. Its combination of plant species, local weather and location give his beasts that little extra in their feed which no agronomist can produce to order. We attach great importance to trace elements, provided they are mineral. More than a few of us ignore the trace elements which are herbal. The pony told me there is more to pasture than just grass. I am grateful for being reminded.

JANUARY 1974

EYE TO EYE

BEYOND THE HALF-DOOR, munching ceased. The ensuing silence seemed louder than the sound had been. From the rain-walk, where I had been putting buckets and brooms into place, I sought reason for the hush. My wife's horse, expert in histrionics, was registering incredulity. His back to the hay net, which was intended to keep him busy for the next hour, amazement permeated every inch of him. His neck had lengthened several inches, for a start. His ears were pricked, his head held high, yet his gaze was focused downwards. Nostrils flared. Shoulder muscles twitched under the satiny skin. He stood as if cornered by some unseen if not unfriendly presence.

Closer inspection proved 'unseen' the wrong word; 'unnoticed' until then was more true. For the presence was that of a mouse. On the tan floor in the opposite corner it had been scavenging cracked oats below the manager.

Evidently the mouse had been as impressed as I was when the horse's munching stopped. Its own munching had done likewise. Oats forgotten, it stared up at the horse as the horse stared down on it. To call it an eyeball to eyeball confrontation might seem far-fetched. The horse's eyeball was larger than the entire mouse. This fact, however, was irrelevant. The scene projected one central question.

'What,' the horse was asking the world in general, 'is that monster doing in here?'

If one thing is more certain than another, it is that the disparity in sizes had not dawned upon the horse. Had that realization been possible, all history would have been different. Man would have had to evolve the world we know without the help of horses. Wars would have been fought wholly on foot. Man's muscle would have been a puny substitute in dragging nourishment from the soil. From the days of Solomon to those of Brunel many great engineering works would have been beyond the power available to humanity.

This failure of horses to make comparisons of heights and mass and draw conclusions is crucial to our domination of them. Being without imagination, they cannot make the deduction which could reverse the relationship. As a boy, this was put to me unforgettably by my grandfather, who did not waste the words which he uttered in his own way. Seeing me in difficulty with a pony, he was not so unwise as to give me help. That would merely have prolonged my problem. Instead he gave me one of life's truths. To some crisp admonition he added:

'He don't know he's bigger and stronger than you are and if I was you I'd pray he never finds out.'

Like the rest of the human race, I have been exploiting that gap in horse sense ever since. But what of the mouse? Horses are not the only species to miss the significance of being either smaller or bigger than others.

Presumably the mouse likewise did not know that it was smaller than the horse. The presence of its giant neighbour therefore did not daunt it. While I watched, the mouse ceased trying to outstare the horse and turned its mind to the more practical matter of the spilled oats, beginning again to forage in the tan. This seemed to relieve the tension for the horse. He turned back to his hay net. Soon the munching recommenced and resumed its confident rhythm.

The episode had occupied about two minutes. On reflection, this seemed too long. The animals had been aware of each other but not, apparently, of me. It would have been perfectly simple for the horse to recognise the presence of the mouse and the mouse to note that of the horse, without either interrupting its meal. It was unlikely that they were strangers. Even if they were, as individuals they cannot have been unfamiliar in a general way. There are often, perhaps always, mice in stables. The co-existence of the two was entirely normal.

Yet the horse's attention had been caught and held by the tiny creature on the floor for as long as that creature met its eye. My guess is that, yet again, the eye was the vital factor. I remembered how I myself had become aware of the mouse. Following the horse's line of sight, my own eyes had been drawn to the area below the manger. And there a needle-point of light had revealed itself. Looking carefully at the spot of light, I saw the rest of the mouse. Light from behind me, over the half-door, was reflecting from its eye.

As with men, so with creatures; the eye is more than an instrument of sight. It is a point of contact not easily broken. Something like a mesmeric effect had been exercised upon the horse, until the moment when the mouse turned its back. Only then could the horse do likewise. Only then, apparently, could it accept the possibility that the loose-box was big enough to hold both of them. No doubt from time to time the mouse is still there. I hope the horse does not feel that its stable companion creates an uncomfortable squash.

JUNE 1981

The Outer World

The outer world is the ring of country round home, its happenings, its sights and sorrows, its memories. It could be any ring of country within sight of any southern English house and village. Perhaps, as is often the sequel to a Proteus essay, several will claim it as their own. If so, part of the author's objective will have been achieved. He does not write of the remarkable, the strange or the tremendous, but of the everyday in which everybody shares.

ROSE OF ENGLAND

NOTHING IN THE lanes is more sudden. One day unsuspected, the next day the first dog rose is there. In my case the day was 6 June. Now we know the summer's shape.

No matter what the solar tables say, the day of the first dog rose is the fulcrum of the season. The tables rule that 21 June is the summer solstice, and so it is. But the zenith in terms of growth is decided only partly by sunshine, and cannot be fore-ordained. Whether or not winter was severe, whether or not spring brought drought, the density and duration of cloud, the rate of change in soil temperature, each has a bearing on the rise of sap, the formation of seed, maturity and decay. To that sequence all our lives are linked. For its common denominator our forefathers picked what is now the floral emblem of the English.

Six weeks after the first dog rose, experienced men told the small boy who once was me, we shall lead harvest. In those days harvests took longer. Instead of the combine grazing off the crop and regurgitating the grain into trailers driven upsides, many pairs of bronzed arms did day-long work behind the reaper. Of all farm jobs, stooking the sheaves was as demanding as any. The stooks stayed out in the sunshine and wind for long enough to be dry enough for stacking. Only then were they pitched on to wains ornate as galleons, and galleon-like as they pitched and swayed across a furrowed stubble, homeward bound. All that would take a week or more.

So now, perhaps, the going date is five weeks after the first dog rose until the grain comes in. That will make it 12 July in our village, allowing an extra day to avoid continuing on Sunday. It looks a fair bet for winter-sown barley, anyway, though much must happen meanwhile. No longer does the weather rule. Wet or dry within reason has only one difference now, the difference between the drier or the silo as first stop from the field. At present my money is on the silo, though we need rain too urgently to joke about it.

Those who chose the dog rose chose well. Like the English it represents, it is not easily deflected from its normal routine. It does not burst impetuously into flower because of rain in May, nor dally merely because there was none in April. It embodies all the factors combined, so as an indicator of an early season or a late one, and how early or late in a particular place, it is trustworthy. Late to come, soon to go, seldom does it appear before Derby day; seldom is it seen after August the Twelfth. So short a stay, so simple a bloom, so important a message, so vigilantly awaited, so very English.

Yet, even having regard to all this, the wonder remains that it ever became a national emblem. Perhaps it would never have done so but for Henry Tudor's flair for public relations when he became King in the aftermath of the Wars of the Roses, and chose a rose for unity. Many of our flowers are more conspicuous, and some more beautiful. The daffodil, claimed by Wales before the prosaic English felt the need, is one. Bluebell, violet, cornflower, poppy and honeysuckle could all stand for England.

Instead the simplest of roses was preferred, transient as it is. It does not dominate the landscape as the candles of the chestnut do, or the whitethorn or the elder flower. Not being visible far off, it must be sought. When found it has the quality of truth. Unlike more prestigious roses, it owes nothing to man's vanity in improving on Nature. It is the genuine species, not the modified one, and it stands for freedom.

Pass by and admire it, but do no more. Pick it for a buttonhole, and it will hang its head in an hour. Even its scent, that distillation of all the sweetness that is England, will leave it. It does not make a complacent captive. In its element on its briar, in an English summer and an English hedge, the dog rose will do for me. It will influence no major transaction, such as those to which a farmer looks forward in marketing his corn. But its presence tells me more than the calendar can about the progress of the season.

It is a time for lifting up the eyes. The valley is unbroken green. Yellowing in less than a month seems too swift for truth. But the dog rose has fixed the date. I do not think it will be wrong.

JUNE 1976

The rose was right. That was the summer of a great drought.

A DRIFT OF DUST

ALL AROUND THE country roars with tractors. Well may the larks sing at heaven's gate. But their voices go unheard amid those of the machines. Across the valley, dark stripes are being drawn on fields pale-faced after winter. Between dawn and dusk hundreds of acres change colour. Near home, the scene can be studied close-up.

Pitching and swaying like a tug at sea, my neighbour's tractor comes head-on towards me. In his weatherproof cab, ear-plugs clamped against bedlam which must be even worse for being confined, he lifts one hand in greeting and clings to his lurching wheel with the other. Behind, the towed cultivator clanks and shudders through the furrows. Its speed would not disgrace a tank in battle. Each tine flings out bow-waves of smashed clods.

Ahead, he judges the narrowing gap between him and our boundary fence. Then, like a yachtsman rounding a buoy, he puts the helm hard over, the whole equipment settles on its new course and a minute later is out of sight, sunk in dead ground, leaving a wake of din and smell and force. But it is not out of earshot. The racket of his engine and the snatch and jerk of metals cannot be lost in a mere 20 acres. Its message will be with us all day.

It tells of ceaseless application of power in an era so out of step with the pace of the land itself that it cannot last for ever. Projecting the mind backwards, it is clear that in comparison with our forefathers we are pushing our luck too far. Projecting it forwards it is difficult to see if, let alone how, our distant descendants can be fed. Every tractor in every field is releasing the energy stored as oil in the crust of the earth while the world was forming. This release is irreversible by our present knowledge. Such energy cannot be recovered, and recycled. It is being expended into the atmosphere not only from nearly every British field, but over much of the globe. The return for it, admittedly necessary, will last humanity just one year. Eventually, its sources will run dry.

The roar of the tractor dies to a static hum. Out of sight, my neighbour must be clearing the cultivator of couch roots. He had better work fast. Another roar, another tractor, is making its presence felt downhill. His son drives this one. It tows the drill, with the farm pupil watching the founts, and behind the drill a triangle of harrows. These purposeful young men will not loiter either.

If synchronization is maintained the governor will just about be in time to unship the cultivator and couple on two rollers in line astern. Positioned precisely earlier in the day, now they wait like relay runners for their turn to come. Then, if he keeps his foot down and treats himself to an hour or so of headlights he will go to bed with the field fully in to barley, and the gate wired-up until spraying time.

For a thousand years, this land knew a different tempo. Instead of three days, the ploughing and tilling and seeding took three months, if not more, worked a little at a time when days could be caught from the weather. Although the harvest thus won would feed fewer mouths, the world was not left the poorer for ever after. From one Plough Monday to another, first the ox and then the horse provided the power which converted the resources of soil, air and water into food acceptable by man, and by the ox and the horse also. They expended no energy which was not in the broad sense recoverable and capable of being repeated. What was taken went back.

Perhaps the long-drawn-out cultivation was less effective, through the long battle with the weather, than the all-out pounding which machines now permit; but populations were smaller. So, probably, were appetites before greed for a supposedly ever-enhanceable standard of living added over-eating to over-population. If man is to turn back and forget his foolish ways, the date when he can bring himself to do so is far off. A reversal now is impossible, when the easy way is still a feasible way, and when the hands of the few are relied upon to fill the mouths of the many others largely employed in making expendable and often superfluous artefacts. But it must come.

We are not likely to be here to see it, and should be thankful for that. Now, in late afternoon as the sun dips on a good day's toil, a rising breeze reveals another cause for gratitude. Dust flies behind the harrows, which is good to see. It means luck to the farmer. He deserves it, even if he serves an improvident world.

MARCH 1977

WITHOUT THE ELMS

CREAK AND CRASH. Another elm tree staggers, leans, and hits the turf. Its branches splinter under a vista of sky where no sky was. Rooks wheel and caw. What fell was their ancestral home. Our own homes, though not fallen, look different now. From the surrounding downs the once plumed village lies bare, its lines unsoftened by the crowns through which the chain-saws have gnawed for weeks. Our elms have become memories.

While hopes remained that perhaps the disease was less real than had been reported, or that it might somehow be cured or contained, we had thought what has happened to be impossible. Who could imagine England without elms? Now we need imagine no longer. We can see. We do not enjoy the new scene. Stark white houses are set in a hard composition of man-made lines and angles. This year there will be no top shade from summer greenery, nor the gold of autumn. The branches which held the leaves are going up in smoke. Raw stumps are their memorials.

So we have decided to replace what we have lost. We shall plant other trees, one for every man, woman and child in the village, all 249 of them. Everybody, from the oldest inhabitant to the baby born just two hours before the list closed, on the last strokes of last year's last midnight, will lend their names to our new trees. We have planned where they shall grow. Each head of a household was asked to help pay for them. There were no backsliders. Such is the effect of trees. No other cause would have produced so much ready cash, nor so little argument. All have had a chance to name a preferred species. Mine is a beech, my wife opts for maple, and our daughters, copper beech and cherry. So the village will begin to see its post-elm age skyline, and a pattern of colours it has never known before.

As years go by, and horizons shorten as Close of Play approaches, I shall look forward to the short walk to my beech tree, to check its progress. By then, with luck, it will be well away. Perhaps the first initials and entwined hearts will have been carved upon its bark, as is the fate of beech trees. So much for prospects.

It will have cost us more than £600 to put in a tree per villager. Foresters would plant for less, because planting more closely and with seedlings. But not all that much more cheaply, and our effort opened my eyes to the funds needed to keep a woodland productive. Because trees are with us for longer than a human lifetime we take them for granted.

Some people create great fuss at their felling. But few, especially in Government seemingly, consider how trees come to be present at all, or how and at whose expense they are cared for across centuries. But unless a tree is to be felled at a time when it is in good health it cannot become part of the useful product of the countryside. To leave it to the downward cycle of old age until, for safety reasons, it has to be thrown as our elms have been, wastes its whole existence. So it is difficult to find common cause with the amiable but distraught ladies who protest at nearly every felling.

Even so, apocalypse was in the air when I walked an oak wood after its timber had been tushed out, the cordwood carted, and the brash burned. Ruts the size of trenches criss-crossed acres of lifeless soil, stamped with black circles of ashes. It was the omega and the alpha of timber, the land's slowest crop. For the first time since the Napoleonic Wars, direct sunshine fell on the forest floor. It brings recovery, and at first the tempo will be fast.

Rosebay (fireweed on Severnside) will glow next autumn. Primroses will bloom next spring. The summer to follow will see bramble back, and pheasants to sunbathe in the low cover. If the owner can afford to put them in, a new generation of young trees should then be there. And if the owner cannot afford it, the result will be what the rest of us cannot afford, either, idle acres. Now, when the elms have gone because of a beetle, is the time to consider which trees will go next because of neglect. Go they will, for one reason or another. Even trees are not immortal. Unless authority makes their replacement justifiable in terms of cost, which is a measure of reality not cupidity, our village a century hence may have its first ever claim to fame – trees, the rarity of the future.

MARCH 1976

CHIEF STARLINGS

SHELTERED IN A dip from a searing easterly, ten acres newly sown to barley rippled as if water overlaid them. Thousands of starlings were in a ritual. Watched through a leafless hedge to a flank, their proceedings at first seemed simple. They fed head to wind, spaced with the usual starling regard for organization. Probing the tilth, they avoided taking each other's ground. But periodically a dozen or two birds took momentarily to wing.

Without breaking formation they would rise about four feet, hover briefly, and return strictly vertically, each to its foraging place. The manoeuvre would be repeated two or three times at intervals of a minute or less. Then others on their boundary did likewise. Up on fluttering wings, short pause, down again to earth, short pause, up on fluttering wings . . . so went the sequence. The next group, and then the next *ad infinitum*, took up the cue. Always they kept the unfailing cohesion of starlings. It became an unbroken chain reaction until the whole flock rose and fell in rhythm like a huge groundsheet rolling out to free its folds.

In the familiar, ever-altering, overcrowded, much-mechanized English countryside there is generally something to see which one has not seen before. But this does not mean that what is seen is new, except to the observer. I did not delude myself that I had made a discovery. Starlings must have behaved thus since the dawn of time. Seeking the why and wherefore, I stopped at a halted tractor. The driver had knocked off from tearing out couch, and was pouring tea from his flask. He was middle-aged, with the wind-scorched face of a man with ample opportunity to see starlings, and much else. Yes; he had sometimes seen them bobbing up and down. Especially when the wind was going over their heads. He thought it might be a way of bringing grubs up to the surface, as blackbirds tread turf to bring up worms.

It sounded feasible. Somebody knows, and somebody will tell me whether or not it is the full truth, or I shall read it eventually. But nobody has told me yet the secret of decision-making in a starling flock. The regular little earth-to-air dance on the feeding ground may well have been spontaneous. But when thousands of starlings are airborne in formation, and travelling to a known destination, some single intelligence must be controlling them. Watch a flock and see the possibilities stemming from indecision, conflicting orders, or distortion in transmitting them.

A big winter flock may be half a mile long. Its components, though not flying quite wing-tip to wing-tip, have little air space. A unilateral five degrees to port or starboard by any one bird would mean collision and pile-up. Never have I seen either, or any other sign of confusion. To change direction means acceleration by the flank on the exterior line, rest at the pivotal point, and proportionate deceleration between the two until the new bearing is reached, and normal speed resumed. It is not enough to say, as doubtless we have all said and thought, as an enormous flock goes over, 'It is their nature so to do'. It remains a very sophisticated piece of flight discipline.

My only first-hand comparable experience lay in commanding three dozen radio-linked military vehicles, driven by far from stupid men, in open order across a desert. I would like to meet an admiral who can tell me of a fleet's signals mechanism, or an air marshal who, being himself airborne, could control the entire war-time strength of the RAF flying in close formation. That, in essence, is what some master starling does every winter's day. That an organizational plan exists is evident from the rehearsal-flights of smaller parties before joining up into a mass formation.

Somewhere in the mass formation must be an especially distinguished starling to whom the destination, the intervening country, and the wind factors are known, and by whom the route is chosen and the course decided. Somehow his messages must be conveyed. Is it, as the time-element would suggest, by thought transference? Somehow, too, he must have been elected, or have elected himself. Somehow he must be recognizable by other starlings; and recognized, or chaos would result and the beautifully ordered flight become a gigantic rabble. Starling rabbles never happen.

Human mass movement lacks polish by contrast. One of the immutable logistics of armed forces is that it is impossible to assemble 200 men without including at least one who is muddle-headed, or absent-minded, or bloody-minded, or suffering from a hangover, or just plain daft, and hence capable, say, of turning full-right when half-right is called for, converting a fly-past into a wizard prang, and a march-past into a shambles. Yet no pack of 10,000 starlings seems to include any such menace.

Starling character seems less than ideal for regimentation. Independent, garrulous, humorous (especially as mimics), and apparently irreverent about life in general, their whole species seems tailor-made for an awkward squad. So my admiration for all supreme-commander starlings is unbounded. I wish I could know one when I meet him.

APRIL 1976

MEN ON A MOUNTAIN

OUR HOSTESS SAID that we must meet each other. Neither of us could have adduced any good reason why. It was one of those things that happen at cocktail parties, and left no way for either of us to avoid the encounter. There followed the verbal sparring which occurs when two male persons are brought into unexpected and unwanted confrontation. Each probed to find some common ground; if that had failed, we would have probed to find each other's weak spot.

Having sized up my man, a bronzed and bearded fellow, firm of shoulder and well co-ordinated, I felt justified in trying one of our neighbourhood's conventional social leads. It is of the when-all-else-fails variety, yet indicates that hope is not extinct, like opening with Two Clubs at bridge.

'Do you farm?' I asked.

It had the desired effect. The necessary doors were unlocked, the common ground revealed. It proved vast in extent. No, he was not a farmer. He was a dentist. What was there about him that suggested agriculture.

His healthy appearance, I replied. That, he said, was temporary only. A week or two in the surgery would reduce him to normality. It came from the Lake District. He had been there for his customary visit, by tradition family-free, able to wander lonely as a cloud, the manner appropriate to those parts.

Once he had said where he had in fact been, we knew metaphorically where we were. Scafell Pike, Helvellyn, Striding Edge, Blencathra and Great Gable tripped fluently from our tongues. The name-dropping became technical. Our hostess had been a pawn in the hand of destiny. We were preordained to meet. Again the spell of high places had spanned the gulf between disparate men. It has happened so often that I have long speculated about this unifying effect of differences in altitude which are in truth generally small. It transcends race, tongue and outlook and is inspired as readily by the small wrinkles on the skin of Britain as by the most stupendous of Himalayan peaks.

It relates to elusive qualities in Nature itself. There is a wide difference between the summit of a mountain and the top of a hill, and it is not a difference of feet or of metres above sea-level. It is indefinable but we know it when we see it. We not only see it, we also feel it. Perhaps its realization stems from difficulties of attainment combined with the character of the scene itself. A mountain arouses a sense only describable as nobility when one stands upon it; a wish to linger and absorb it, a reluctance to turn one's back and go down. A hill does none of these things. It is a mere element in a planned transition, not an achievement in itself. A hill gives us nothing; a mountain does. We remember for ever each separate ascent, even amid the deafening buzz of a cocktail party.

Not that a mountain top is necessarily noble in itself. The minor cairns of rusting beer cans, now a feature of most of those in Britain, are in themselves unlovely sights. Yet they, too, arouse in men of mountains that sense of kinship with others of the brotherhood who have come, breathed-in the spirit of the lonely height, slaked their thirst and gone. Hence the absence of barrier, let alone friction, between those who meet on mountains, or talk about them afterwards. Even the most reserved of men disclose personal details unprompted, as if of the listener's right, especially when celebrating the moment of triumph by eating the simple piece which climbers carry. Not merely the immediate view, breathtaking though it invariably is, but the world itself grows larger.

In loosing the strings of the tongue, *wurst* seems especially effective. On Hohemunde in Tyrol the only other occupant of its final comb of rock was a massive German whose collection of memento badges had overflowed his hat and encrusted also his *Lederhosen*. Together we masticated the Teuton's universal fortifier. Unasked, he told me his name and that of the company of which he was president, the profits it was making, why it made them, and where he thought its English competititors missed opportunities. I could offer little in return except my name and domicile, and the ages and characteristics of my offspring. Such being life on mountain summits, the exchange was sufficient and great was the handshaking before we returned by separate routes to our normal levels.

Only once have I encountered even the seeds of discord on a mountain. I had climbed Skiddaw from Millbeck, a short, sharp ascent which throws a new and more exciting light on that much loved but rather prosaic mountain. During the last traverse across outward sloping slabs gleaming with the wetness of low cloud, I could see that the summit was already tenanted. Six large and youngish men, weather-beaten, craggy-faced, evidently thirsty, girt with ropes and wearing woolly hats, regarded me blank faced as I reached their level. 'We been watching yow coom oop,' said their spokesman heavily, in the flat accents of northern England. 'What you got in yon pannier?'

The question seemed intrusive, almost as if spoken by a Customs officer rather than a casual acquaintance in beatific surroundings. I eased the pack from off my back. Six pairs of eyes scrutinised it closely. 'We thowt you'd maybe brought nipper oop.' Truth dawned. The pack was one of those designed for carrying young children. My new companions were absentee fathers, and wished to remain so. Confirmation followed.

'If tha'd brought nipper oop, and word got round,' declared the first speaker as he deftly flicked a personal contribution on to the beer-can cairn, 'we'd all be bringing nippers oop before you could spit.'

'Aye, and wives,' added the party's pessimist, 'they're better back in Keswick, even if they are spending brass.'

'Nay women aboov Cat Bells,' pronounced the spokesman with finality. One sensed that there were audiences to which he would not have said it. Hence part of the magic of high places.

As the talk turned to other matters the last of the now tattered cloud-wrack passed over. We family men were left surrounded by the sky's clear blue, and aware of being nearer than usual to the sun. Not just to the sun, perhaps.

NOVEMBER 1981

VOICE OF THE TOAD

THE VOICE OF the toad had more than one message. To me it said, 'Behold, I show you a mystery.' For the other toad, which it addressed, the meaning was more elemental. A year had passed since I discovered that we are hosts to a natterjack. He and I met at dusk last summer on a flight of shallow steps leading to the house. His dart into cover caught my eye before I knew what he was.

Too substantial to be a shrew, too deliberate for vole or woodmouse, too smooth a mover to be a frog, investigation was demanded. Having made my last rounds, I had a torch. Its beam revealed him, a dapper figure by toad standards, poised alert under a trailing spray of American pillar rose.

Few people, it seems, have knowingly seen a natterjack. The name generates amusement, and the assumption of rarity which I doubt exists. There are places where natterjacks are less uncommon, and more often seen, than the so-called common toad, though seldom recognised because those seeing any toad for the first time assume it to be the common variety. Misidentification in reverse is impossible. The grotesque common toad, of the earth earthy, dull and warty of skin, ungainly in gait, cannot be confused by those who have seen both with the smarter appearance of a natterjack. Even in torchlight my natterjack was an elegant study in golden-striped, multi-spotted olive.

For two minutes or so we weighed each other up. Then he nipped across the step on which we stood, vanishing nimbly into a crevice where the next rise joined. The manner of his going cancelled all doubt. Not the laboured hopping of common toads, nor the vaulting athleticism of a frog, just a fluent run, more like a mammal than a reptile. It was the first of many meetings, always on the flight of steps. His hide-out was evidently beneath them.

Before the rains came this summer I heard him calling. Therein lay the mystery. A natterjack lifts up his voice and speaks only in one circumstance, the prelude to procreation. A natterjill is for ever silent. Like frogs, toads fertilize and lay their spawn in water. There the tadpoles hatch in late summer, swimming until their legs are formed and they become land-based. But in which water?

There are few acres in the parish where my foot does not fall at some time in the year. I know where water is, and is not. In only one place within its boundaries can moorhens be seen. That is a farm pond, two and a half miles away. Another farm pond, which dries out in summer, is a mile away. Our winterbourne, also dry in summer, is half a mile off. There are two goldfish pools in village gardens, but not within a quarter of a mile of us. There is a well, long unused and concrete-capped, on our ground; when last measured the water was 117 feet down.

So the mystery narrowed to where the dweller beneath the steps proposed to initiate another natterjack generation. There is no doubt that is what he had in mind. His trilling call, musical though slightly hoarse, greeted me at my own gate on an evening heavy with dews. We wanted much more and I was lamenting the lack of rain when the first whistle came. Its origin was difficult to locate, as often happens with such sounds as birdsong or a vixen's yelp in the echo-producing surroundings of chalk hillside. So I stalked the whistle from different bearings, moving here and there as it continued at intervals for fifteen minutes or so. Every audition brought me back to the stone steps. Eventually I stood on them as he trilled beneath my feet. At times we would give much for garden water. There are perennials and shrubs which we could grow if we had it. With a divining rod and the natterjack's help I traced a faint water signal indicating beneath the steps.

If the natterjack had showed us one mystery, he had solved another. For years we have wondered at the number of frogs on our high-lying, quick-drying, often dessicated ground. Clean, prosperous, cheerful frogs, their moist skins gleaming with well-being, leap in the grass under the apple trees when we pick in autumn, 500 yards in distance and 200 feet in altitude from the nearest garden pool. Though we bemoan our supposedly barren land, it seems that there is water under it. Beyond our sight and knowledge, presumably in darkness, enough is lying for natterjacks to contemplate breeding, perhaps for frogs to have bred. What food resources can exist in the absence of light is beyond conjecture.

In earth, air and water life is full of unknown quantities. There are more beneath our feet than ever we know. If the future brings us more natterjacks, the mystery of our unseen pool will have grown.

JULY 1982

BEES, PAST AND PRESENT

ONE WAVERING BEE briefly joined the sleepy wasps in the autumn sunshine, gorging themselves on a last plum, election-ripe. Then the bee flew on. As an organisation bee, he had to report back to the hive. The wasps stayed out longer.

On the face of it, to be a bee is preferable to being a wasp as winter approaches. Bees have material advantages. The hegemony of the human race ensures they do not starve nor, other than in exceptional weather, freeze. In comparison, wasps live to the standards of a banana republic. Their nests are vulnerable to hazards ranging from epicurean badgers to passing bulldozers. Provision for the future, by their own efforts solely, seems to be on a hit-or-miss basis.

Nevertheless, I would rather be reincarnated as a wasp than a bee. Despite their excellent housing, the life-style of the bees has unattractive characteristics. I have had brief insights into it. The pervasive emphasis on production, without proportionate reward for the producer and involving a policy of all work and no play, is in itself unattractive. One suspects a rip-off. The existence of a small privileged élite, permanently unemployed except for their function in establishing the leadership, makes one think nervously of Britain under Mr. Benn.

Not only do I believe that wasps have more fun, more freedom, more scope for self-determination, fewer rules and less strait-jacketed democracy than bees, but I also believe that bees' way of life equates all too closely to communism. Not that I have lived under a communist régime, except, for practical purposes, in the Army. And, since I was then one of the commissars, it is possible that the life was less unprepossessing for me than for others.

Having a greater regard for apiarists than for the bees themselves, the chance has come for me to see the inside of hives from time to time. The experience is daunting, in some respects resembling that of fraternal delegates at a stroppy union meeting. One feels less than wholly welcome. There are the same ominous murmurings and agitated comings and goings. The similarities go further. No matter what the workers want, the leadership gets its way in the end. Individuals have no status, except to do what they are told. And the part played by smoke, if not smoke-screens, heightens the similarity.

Nevertheless, those of us who peer into these matters must concede the great services which bees render to the human race. Honey, the most obvious, is less totally beneficial than pollination. Without bees, many harvests would have been denied us by our own insecticides, especially in orchard fruit. So when the weather breaks, and I pass the hives clustered in field corners, and now revealed by the die-back of surrounding plants, I wish their inmates well in the storm and the tempest, the frost and snow to come. My wishes extend to their owners, too. Bee-keeping is costly nowadays, as well as scientific. Much capital is tied up in a couple of dozen hives. In a way I am sorry about this. When capital enters in, romance goes out, even from an enterprise rooted on communist principles. Modern progress, less colourful traditions, even the traffic, have changed the face of bee-keeping.

No longer does the rising generation enjoy the exhilarating pursuit of swarms which was a feature of my boyhood and the next best thing to foxhunting. To keep the swarm in sight was an important element in establishing ownership when it eventually came to rest. Hence my memories of a blissful day in my first decade, culminating in an early half-crown.

Exerting energy like Willie Carson on a racehorse, I propelled my bicycle hell-for-leather down a village street with the Clee in the background, ringing the bell and squeaking 'Mr. Gould's bees!' as often as I had breath. The black cloud which on departure had loomed large and ominous, and sounded like an aeroplane, became tantalisingly small as it swirled and became tattered over adjacent gardens. At times only the last wisps of it, its stragglers doubtless panting in the bee manner as much as I was, remained in sight.

It would be death for a small boy to do it now. But then it was possible. All knew the object of the exercise. The street could not have been more thoroughly cleared for John Gilpin himself, the mere name of Mr. Gould carrying great weight locally, and I was up and able to mark them to tree in the garden of a rather grand lady who said, when I gasped out my message, 'Well, tell Mr. Gould to take the horrible things away.'

In due course Mr. Gould came, with measured tread, and garbed in splendour. No coward soul was his; no veils and gloves came between him and his beloved bees. In spotless flannels and the blazer of an eminent cricket club, he talked, cajoled and shook the bees down into a sack, then strode off home with them, readily avoided by all and sundry. As for me, I was enriched by the experience, not only by the half-crown, and just one bee among the wasps on a rotten plum was enough to bring the memory back.

OCTOBER 1978

HARE OF ILL OMEN

ON THE HEADLAND of a spring-sown barley field a far-off object which was shaped yet shapeless posed the question, Animate or inanimate? It had not been there on the previous evening. Now, a strange mixture of the angular and the crumpled, it towered above the seedling spears, stunted by the wait for rain.

From 100 yards away its material composition was a matter of guesswork. Metal, perhaps – a squashed petrol tin fallen off the back of a lorry on the adjoining road. Or plastic, the wind-twisted remnant of a rick cover blown there overnight. Or a bundle of discarded hessian, lying where it dropped. By now the range had closed to 50 yards, then 40. Having seen such a miracle previously, I was not unduly surprised to find my assumption of inanimate falsified. For this strange thing, so dark and hunched and in which no line or attitude of Nature could be seen, suddenly transformed itself into a lithe and sandy-coloured hare.

All clean lines and sinewy rhythm, it turned across my line of approach to give me a full monocular lateral inspection, the hare's equivalent of looking a man squarely in the eye. Then, ears erect, it accepted that its morning doze was over. At a relaxed 25 mph it cruised away. Typical of hares. The sun had been up a short hour. Another hare had been caught out in a normally unharelike situation. There seems no limit to their indiscretions.

This hare had no doubt fed well during the night. Life is easy now, with growth in progress everywhere. No doubt, too, a short browse along the tops of the tender barley rows made an agreeable final delicacy to round off the menu. And then, presumably at peace with the world, this hare just nodded off where he happened to be at the time.

Six feet away was the metalled lane. Perhaps the day was still too young for traffic, but traffic there would surely be within a few minutes of my unscheduled arrival. The Post Office van with the letters, and cars bringing farm hands to their work, would all be bound for the village to which the lane led. The hare had evidently been unimpressed by this likelihood. Yet no creatures have better eyes and noses for country than hares, which well know the areas to avoid. Their tracks and smeuses take the safest ways. Though they must often cross roads, and sometimes fall victim to traffic, they do not normally ask for trouble by offering themselves for inspection.

This confirms my doubts about the hare's reputation for madness, a fair and longstanding example of rural half-truth. It stems from the standard mixture of countrymen's accurate observation and countrymen's accompanying inability to analyse and deduce. Lapses of prudence by hares, as in the present instance, suggest failure to maintain concentration rather than the legendary insanity. The more one learns about hares, the move evident that they are highly intelligent creatures. But high intelligence does not preclude absent mindedness, among professors, for example. There is no doubt that in certain circumstances the normally prudent and circumspect hare, with all its highly sensitised apparatus for self-preservation, allows its attention to wonder.

These occasions seem to me to be related to times when life is good for hares. Their famed and obvious loss of discretion in March is a case in point. While the bucks dance around and pursue their chosen does, and box each other, they adopt a devil-may-care attitude, casting their customary secretiveness aside, oblivious of who may see. The customary reason given for this is their mating season, said to be at or about that month. While I accept that in the spring a hare's fancy may lightly turn to thoughts of procreation, I find this explanation too simplistic. Facts do not support it.

The hare has no mating season. Leverets are born at all seasons of the year, including midwinter. Though more are born, and more survive, in summer than at other times, this does not establish spring as a mating season. But spring is indeed a time when pleasures loom. The struggle for existence being eased, hares can then turn their minds to different matters, especially if pleasurable. An increased incidence of this, and of absent mindedness, are separate and distinct consequences, not the causes, of hares' attitudes of mind in March, or at any other time.

To perform their rituals in public, or to be asleep in full view of a moving man, are not typical acts of hares during the rest of the year. At other times they are gone with the wind, or clap, with the hares' genius for self-effacement. In doing so, they act in conformity with their reputation for disquieting, magical, sometimes sinister ways.

The hare – the graceful, gentle, innocent hare, with no defence against a world of enemies except secrecy and speed – is even now surrounded by ill omen for humanity. All our sophistication, education and communication have not yet dispelled it. Its sudden ways have made it supernatural. The hare is there, and then it is not. Or it is not there, and then it is. It materialises out of nothing, and vanishes into nothing. An old sack develops limbs and ears, and disappears at speed. It crosses people's paths, especially those of women in the gloaming, unforgettable even to those who profess disbelief in it as a harbinger of misfortune.

Beaters who at the end of the day's shooting gladly take a rabbit home, do not care or do not dare to take a hare under their roof. Nor are they reluctant to say so. In logic there is no foundation for the nameless fears which attach to hares all round the world. Indian soldiers much disliked meeting a hare on their night patrols. Once I asked them why. The hare sat in the moon, they said. I knew what they meant. I was warned about hares long since by less imaginative folk. Hares are unkit, we used to say in Shropshire, leaving it at that.

MAY 1982

WINTERBOURNE

THROUGH MOST OF March the westerlies blew. They scooped up Atlantic vapour and dropped it on us. Day after day the rain fell. Ditches were waterlogged. Lanes were flooded. But the winterbourne stayed dry.

Those villagers senior enough to be listened to on so elemental a subject reckon that the winterbourne flows once in three years. A five-year gap is exceptional, a matter for long and frequently adjourned debates in the bar, and probably still unspoken speculations as to whether some dire sin has been committed which has led to the denial of this symbol of man's most basic need. Now it is eight winters since the bourne flowed, bringing with it excitement and upheaval in our lives. When it happens, school children gather on the bridge, which spans what normally seems a dry ditch. Householders along the banks take up panic stations. Those most threatened arm themselves with prongs and stand by to clear the flotsam which builds up above the bridge, swept down until arrested by the brambles which have grown since the last eruption.

Our winterbourne is no mere channel for flood water. It is one of the veins in the earth's circulatory system which happens to lie skin deep, as it were, instead of far underground as most of them do. It does not flow because its channel has been filled from above, but because water has been forced up from underneath. Then for once in a while, we see an aquifer in action, one of the natural conduits which prevent the chalk counties drying out into semi-desert. The winterbournes (the name recurs across the maps wherever there is downland) give us occasional views of themselves. The rest of the aquifers, a much greater number, flow perpetually unseen, unheard, deep beneath our feet.

When our winterbourne flows we call it the breaking of the springs. The springhead is a mile or so above the village. A cottage stands 100 yards away, inhabited by a local sage of gypsy stock. He acts as a self-elected high priest of the springs, and relates graphically what happens when they break.

'You hears it a'coming,' he says. 'Then you feels it, like a wind from underground. Then you hears it again, with them puffing and a'sighing like an old cow. Then the water comes. Ah, 'tis terrible, terrible.'

But, here, in otherwise waterlogged Wessex, we have not heard it yet. With water lying all around, the winterbourne itself does not hold a spoonful. Significantly, this is our state at winter's end, after the wettest March for years.

Far back in time, the Saxon founders of the village must have looked carefully with experienced eyes at the winterbourne. Water was their criterion in choosing where to put down their roots. If they had it, they trusted to their muscle power to enable crops to grow; but no amount of effort could produce water if none was available. The presence of the winterbourne proved that some was. Down its course, where the valley opened out and gave space for communal fields, they sank new wells and the village grew around them. We, their successors and some of us perhaps their heirs, consider that they chose well.

Whether they would have made the same choice, if, in their day, the winterbourne had been as dry after so much rain, is anybody's guess. That great and suspicious changes have taken place in the waters under the earth is plain to us now. The land must have been robbed of much of its natural reserve of water if, after eight long years, and months of repeated deluge, there is not yet enough to break our springs.

MARCH 1977

Comedies of Manners

As certainly as seasons change, so do social customs; and, like the seasons, they repeat themselves in sequence. So we have the oddities of social life, some in advance of their time, others behind it. The sure conclusion is that, if we could live long enough, we should have seen it all before, because in human affairs there is nothing new under the sun. It is in their verities that the scenes related here touch us all, marking us and our generation as late twentieth-century country folk, our small changes in custom and behaviour reflecting the social revolution which we British have successfully disguised.

NIGHT OF THE VANDALS

RUDDY IN THE village streets of Britain, telephone boxes retain their familiar hue. The decision not to paint them yellow gave me pleasure. That this was ever suggested may reflect the strange stresses of our era which make psychiatry so thriving an industry. Perhaps some functionary, deeply enmeshed in tele-communication and crazed by contemplation of the preposterous Buzby as its emblem, felt his sanity threatened by a compulsive desire for change. This could well have been sublimated into a plan for mammoth vandalism through official channels. What greater vandalism could be imagined than painting every telephone box yellow?

Telephone boxes and vandalism seem inseparable. Why this should be mystifies me. A telephone box is above reproach as a useful installation, of value to the whole community, especially in emergency, fulfilling the most respectable of left wing ideals by serving all men according to their needs. It can be used by those of all races, pigmentation, religions and, doubtless most importantly, trade unions. It can be, and frequently is, occupied by more than one person at a time, being notably innocent of sex discrimination. Its facilities do not stop at mere communication, a secondary role in rubbish disposal being widely recognised.

However, the spoliation of telephone boxes is a recreation now much practised in the countryside; though not always, I dare to think, by country people. It happens too often to be called any longer a phenomenon. It once brought me an experience (the only one so far in a sheltered life) of vandalism in action.

I was homeward bound on a long, winter car journey; darkness had fallen. The time had come to ring my family, partly to reassure them of my continued existence, partly to transmit an estimate of when I might require nourishment. Since this is a need which often arises, I have developed a keen eye for telephone boxes and for appreciating swiftly the vandalisation factor.

Crossing the Severn, I put myself on alert. All round Gloucester only a slight easing of speed was needed to absorb the signs. Telephone box doors hung open, revealing wreckage within. Two were occupied, one of them by two persons engaged in unspecified activity (they might already have telephoned). From Birdlip into Cirencester two more were occupied and another vandalised. Vandalism at some causes overcrowding at other telephone boxes still intact. Then, approaching the now lost town of Swindon, hidden beyond the strange by-passes and ramparts of the hidden city of Thamesmead, the headlights picked up the scene for which I hoped.

Here was a box all in one piece. No broken panes were evident at first sight. It was fully illuminated. The handset was in place, a directory on its shelf. An idyllic sight indeed. In short, it had not been vandalised. But by the time I had stopped the car, parked it and walked back it had been. Two vandals, callow beneath their helmets and leather jackets, were pulling out the last inches of flex as I arrived. Five more sat around on motor-cycles, engines running.

My words, carefully chosen, were for that reason inaudible. But the senior vandal was no dead loss at lip reading. He roared an order to cut their engines; then 'Say it again, squire', he invited.

I did, offering my opinion that they had done a damn silly thing; I wanted to use that phone, I said. In the headlight glare of passing cars, no eye met mine. They seemed stunned at the realization that a telephone box might be in demand for such a purpose. Well, I asked, where was the next nearest phone box. No answers. 'Stratton St. Margaret?' I suggested. 'That one don't work,' said a flex-puller, with the confidence born of certain knowledge.

A voice from the back named a village unknown to me, and now forgotten. How far? I asked. About three mile. How did I get there? Conversation now loosening up, explanations were many and incomprehensible. I appealed for a single spokesman.

'Tell you what, squire,' said the senior vandal, 'we'll take you there'. And they did. Kick starters went into action. With four in front and three behind as escort, we roared through complex lanes. I learned how the American president travels.

The telephone box was pristine. No sign of onslaught here. Will this do? the vandals asked, showing it off with pride, like estate agents offering a house for sale. Do it did. Floodlit by the headlights of the seven motor-cycles, I made my call.

Where to now? was the question when I emerged and thanked them. Marlborough next, I said. He'll need to go through the village and fork right, volunteered the local expert. We'll take him, ruled the ever-reliable senior vandal.

The unknown village reverberated again to the roaring engines. Surrounded by successive glare and shadows from the swerving headlights, and the appalling noise, we swung along yet more lanes and filtered through to the by-pass. For a mile they rode around my car, still like a guard of honour, then accelerated away. Their rearlights receded down the south-bound track, magnetised by ton-up glory.

They were still in sight when, as seven pricks of light far ahead, they circled the M4 intersection. Then their headlights came streaming back along the other carriageway. I flicked my own lights in salute and we passed out of each other's lives. With any luck we had all learned something. Anyway, they had demonstrated that 'nothing better to do' is a phrase with a practical application.

AUGUST 1981

A Post Office plan to change the colour of telephone boxes had been abandoned in face of public outcry.

MALICE AFORETHOUGHT

HUMAN NATURE INCLUDES guile, vindictiveness, perfidy, chicanery and spite. Since nothing is evolved without purpose, some may wonder what part these attributes fulfil in the general scheme of things. To me it is self-evident that they exist as fundamentals for the delicious and ruthless game of croquet. No form of contest is more misunderstood. In vulgar minds the traditional 'game of croquet at a vicarage garden party' is a synonym for endeavour of a milk-and-water kind. Those who believe this can have scant experience of vicarage garden parties, which are no environment for fainthearts, and none of playing croquet. If the image survives of the prototype croquet player as being a maiden lady of gentility and seniority, none should under-estimate the arsenic-and-old-lace syndrome. In fact, of course, the great game is played by every sort and condition, including male persons of virile, aggressive, and even gorilla-like aspect.

Though it seems to be regarded as a rare eccentricity by those who broadcast or write in newspapers, my belief is that croquet has lately gained much in popularity. And so it should. As a means of exercising those resources of fret and choler which we all possess, and which cannot otherwise be usefully deployed in civilised society, croquet transcends all other activities. In grace and poise it contrasts favourably with the contorted violence of golf, in mathematical combination it challenges chess, in accuracy and delicacy it compares with snooker, and in conversational possibilities it would make mincemeat of the Congress of Vienna.

My pleasure this summer has been to return to the lawn, and to discover that the less admirable traits of my character have not grown rusty by under-employment. Two decades had elapsed since last I took mallet in hand and, dismissing their playing skill as of small consequence, weighed-up the psychological weaknesses of the opposition. The click as blue was sent on its way was as the sound of the trumpet to a war horse. Our family had a croquet tradition. One forbear played it almost non-stop from To Finish the Season until cub-hunting, declaring it to be the only reasonable summer pastime for a foxhunter too old for cricket. He played it, moreover, with the disregard for ethics and mastery of the underhand which make croquet what it is.

The dissemination of alarm and despondency among the enemy (at croquet they are not mere opponents), the nurturing of doubt and bewilderment, demand histrionic art and a sense of timing once the perquisite of high diplomacy. The tactical conferences between partners, when voices are lowered to invite eavesdropping, and then raised enough to release an inspired leak, could teach Whitehall a thing or two. An impassive ox-like stare when an opponent is bent on mischief is the stuff of which trade union leaders are made. All human life is there.

What happens to the balls and mallets, hoops and pegs is no more than the thread which binds great ploys together. Croquet is a game of baleful plotting and hostile imagination. The spoken word and the unuttered inference are its true currency. Nobody should play croquet who lacks a sense of humour. So said one of our croquet-hosts this summer. He understated. Nobody should be allowed to play croquet who is likely to abide by a sense of chivalry or magnanimity. Such would be too dull a fellow to engage the attention of those of more liberal views. Ladies who take part should be possessed of barbed and acid tongues, and a gift for distracting laughter, especially if young and attractive.

Given these ingredients, plus a suitable side bet and a lawn which plays true while not devoid of interesting borrows, the scene is set for an English afternoon of idyllic rancour, especially if there are beeches in the background and tea in the offing. Should the next world offer croquet I hope my wife and I can take on Al Capone and Lucrezia Borgia. They would be in their element. Their side-talk might be interesting, and it would be a pleasure to dispatch them to those distant zones from which (except at upstage places like Roehampton and Cheltenham) the road back is long and hazardous.

SEPTEMBER 1973

THE GENTLER CRICKETERS

MY WIFE LIT upon a diagram in some publication which told her, for the first time in her life, the placings of the fielders at cricket. As the scales fell from her eyes, permitting her thenceforth at last to view the great game in full comprehensibility, my own feelings were of mingled amazement, indignation and guilt.

Amazement, that I had been living in connubial bliss with one who had not known long-on from gully. Indignation, that her family, replete with well-informed males, had left her in ignorance; her father should surely have found a moment to take her on one side and tell her. Guilt, that I myself had not done so. Like most men, I am not tongue-tied about cricket. My comments when some match (who cares whom it is between) is the stuff of television are, I hope, an illuminating supplement to those of Mr. Benaud and his mellow friends. For years my spouse's acceptance of them in uncontesting silence had seemed to me to indicate that their pertinence left no more to be said. Now I know different.

Aware, as she now is, of the significance behind such previously occult terms as square leg, third man and mid-on, her own contribution can be expected. And not only hers, presumably, since feminine eyes up and down the realm will have lit upon that very diagram whose message, apparently, was not the sort of thing that every woman knows – anyway not until now. A whole new technically with-it phalanx of cricket critics is about to materialise in the homesteads of our land.

This being so, reflections upon the chain of cause and effect raise questions. Why should it be happening only now? Cricket has been played for centuries. Why, indeed, should the idea of publishing the diagram have entered anybody's head? Unless, of course, there was space to fill and nothing else to fill it with. Who would have imagined the necessity to explain any aspect of cricket to a sizeable section of the British public? The assumption has always been that there are matters on which we Britons do not require instruction and cricket is one of them. If we are not foreigners, which means people who do not play cricket, we are born well-informed about it.

As surely as we shed our milk-teeth, the knowledge grows within us of where silly point stands (and in most cases so does a natural reluctance to stand there ourselves) and kindred realizations about third man, the multiplicity of slips and extra cover. The same is true of those born in Australia and New Zealand, South Africa, the Caribbean islands and the Indian sub-continent.

In my own family, the minor circumstance of being born feminine was not held to interfere with this. When a quorum was available and leisure coincided, those on the distaff side were expected to put down their distaffs and mix whitewash to mark out the wicket. Toleration was not accorded to any conscientious objectors seeking excuse from the ensuing conflict.

She who was dispatched to mid-off, for example, was permitted her 'What, me?' but not 'Where is it?' Cold feet were forgivable, just; cluelessness was not, even in face of the most ferocious of batsmen.

In this respect, the field placings at family and village cricket have diminished significance. The right blend of intimidators and humourists in the slips and a preponderance of youth in the outfield to counteract the non-benders close in, are the main requirements at the grass roots. But in this simplicity there is a trap for the unwary. Like most games, cricket becomes easier at its advanced levels. Where pitches are perfect, stroke play conventional and bowling true to type, unknown quantities are few. A particular ball to a particular batsman can be hit to cover point, for example, or nowhere. The element of surprise is rare.

In cricket at my level, anything can happen. And generally it does, especially to me. Not for us the apparent magnetising of the clean-struck ball which gives the first-class game its air of predestination and decorum. In our circles the crimson rambler approaches at speeds and angles of infinite variety. Sometimes it comes in the guise of projectile, sometimes elusively with hops and skips. In either case defence in depth may well be needed. The human element can be found wanting.

My own position as wicket-keeper is a case in point. I have farmed it as a kind of pocket borough for several decades now and the reason is well-known to all, though tactfully muted in conversation. Only there, condemned to constant vigilance by the threat of physical injury, can I be relied upon not to be lost in contemplation of the pigeons on the barn roof when a moment of crisis comes. Diagrams or no diagram, one prosaic duty unites most of those romantic-sounding entities typified by backward short leg, long leg, fine leg, point and even long stop. It is merely to remain awake. Only at the really prestigious heights are such persons rendered sleepless by anxiety.

JULY 1981

JACK POINT

SUSPICION BECOMES CERTAINTY as he lowers his shoulders against a straw bale, lies otherwise full length, tips his cap over his half-closed eyes and, even from his prone position, surveys the company loftily. These movements betray that Jack Point among shooting guests, the man who says he never eats lunch. We have all met him. In various guises he is distributed over Britain on a scale of about one per District Council area. Not for him the basket, the sandwich tin, the rustle of greaseproof paper, the pop of corks, the hard-boiled eggs and the apples which escape the grasp and roll elusively into the stubble. 'Lunch?' he exclaims, as of some eccentricity of which he has dimly heard, 'Never have any myself.' And he leaves the rest of us to dig our graves with our teeth.

Such, anyway, is the theory. Seldom does it work out in practice. A genuine Jack Point, who sips no sup and craves no crumb, and weakens not in the hour of temptation, has yet to cross my path. It is an innocent pleasure to watch destiny work out its established course.

Ladies are present. What will happen is therefore obvious. The one spectacle in Nature which is anathema to ladies is the sight of a man not eating. Their compulsion to feed him is as overpowering as that which enslaves a pair of dunnocks in the presence of a fledgling cuckoo. Four of them bend their gaze upon the supine form. His is a personable figure, not suggestive of privation. A rotundity at the top of the knickerbockers cannot be denied. Lunch or no lunch, had any of them been married to him steps would have been taken to alter that. As it is, the landscape is marred by a non-masticating male figure. The question is, Whose move? The pecking order, of course, must be honoured.

'Oh, come on,' says the wife of the managing Gun, 'you can't go without anything at all.' Reflecting that I would not care to be asked to parse that sentence, nor answer for its logic, I note an easing of the posture ready for that which he is about to receive. 'Here, try a slice of our grouse pie,' goes on the lady bountiful, 'just a thin slice won't kill you, you know.' Nor does it. He requires little more pressing when the jolly wife of the landowner picks up the theme. With the delicate air of one not wishing to give offence, he accepts the buttered toast on which calories in the form of pâté have been generously heaped. 'Have some salad to go with it,' invites the third lady, deftly mobilizing plastic plate, lettuce, tomatoes, cucumber, young onions, diced potato, mayonnaise. 'Rather against my principles, you know, ' declares Jack Point, unconvincingly. He is now bolt upright.

Principles or not, he puts up no resistance when the young soldier's wife discovers a bath chap surplus to establishment.

'Can't take it home, can we?' she suborns. They cannot, indeed. 'Years since I had one,' remarks a grateful Jack Point. He has now put away rather more than anybody else, and correspondingly appreciates the glass of ale which willing hands are propelling in his direction, to be followed in due course by coffee, and cherry brandy.

To impute parsimony would be unfair. He is much too nice a man for that. Moreover, his intention must be judged genuine. To attempt to live off the country by relying on the generosity of others would be a risky gamble. Its success infers a mixed party. Most men, taking him at his word, would leave him to his fate.

Moreover, many of us will sympathize with his basic motive. Having enjoyed many noble shooting lunches, and being hopeful of enjoying many more, I remain unconvinced of their place in the agenda. A day's sport, says my personal philosophy, should leave a man with appetite sharpened, not replete. Yet to healthy constitutions, as are those of outdoor people, good fare hospitably prepared is not something from which to turn one's head. Those of us who in hard times dined for weeks on end by taking in our belts two holes have a lifelong incentive to down our sherry and turn to the table. Only afterwards do doubts return.

Which among us does not know the feeling that all is not well when, climbing into the Land-Rover for the traditional high moment, the first drive after lunch, we realize that the day is two shades darker than it ought to be? Our sport cannot now keep step with the count-down which Nature pegs to the onset of dusk. Something has become out of hand. We all know what.

So I lean a little towards Jack Point; just far enough to see the attractions of a day planned too far from home to be able to go in to lunch. On such occasions my own pleasure would be a slice of fruit cake, and apple and cheese, a bottle of beer. Ample room would remain in the bag for cartridges. On our own small shoot we invariably go in to lunch; but never come out again. One does not need to be a Jack Point to keep going until 2.30, especially if flasks of soup have intercepted the party after the midday drive. And early afternoon seems late enough on a winter's day.

OCTOBER 1975

MOURNING THE MOUSTACHE

UNDER THE FORTHRIGHT gaze of some rarely seen ancestral portraits my thoughts turned to a national decadence. They concerned the sorry state which now afflicts that once inspiring feature, the British moustache. In its former richness and diversity it typified a virile nation. But many of my fellow citizens have become content to resemble consumptive Mexicans. Their drooping, ill-kempt, supralabial hair turns inward and downward at the corners of the mouth. The effect is a gaunt, devitalized, half-starving impression.

Others favour beards which are allowed to rampage untrimmed. These bestow on their proprietors a weak, defensive air, as of men for ever peering apologetically over blackthorn hedges. Failure in beardmanship, however, may be passed over lightly. Unlike the moustache, the beard has not been a feature deeply entrenched in the British way of life. Seafarers alone have taken to it unselfconsciously. Even there, doubt obscures the motivation. Perhaps it is for warmth, and thus even more necessary now that grog has been discontinued. Perhaps it is mere lack of dexterity with the razor in ships rolling and pitching across the storm-lashed oceans.

Except among a few enthusiasts the beard can hardly be regarded as an art form. The moustache certainly is one. To arrest its decadence, the Ministry of the Environment should step in. It has stepped in on less worthwhile grounds. To consider, as I did, the faces of past generations is to mourn what we have lost. Where now can be seen the baroque rhythms of Dundreary whiskers in combination with unshaven lip but shaven chin? The pressures of modern life preclude such time-consuming cultivations. More is the pity.

In addition to much else, we owe the Royal Air Force gratitude for a brief renaissance in moustache development during the Second World War. Their officers reintroduced that hallmark of masculinity, the handlebar. Many such moustaches achieved impressive spans, sweeping to port and starboard like the horns of a buffalo. Not every man can carry off the handlebar effect as to the manner born, any more than every man can fly aircraft in battle. Both demand buoyancy of spirit, and attention to detail. Much brushing is needed to obtain lustre, since the handlebar must be couth, without loss of droop resistance. Only the dedicated attempt it, and dedication is rare. Rather less demanding was the cavalry version. This was slightly shorter in the beam, and brushed upward at the extremities. The effect was to add a dash of arrogance to the manly virtues conferred by the handlebar.

The rural scene especially has been poorer for the obsolescence of the erstwhile badge of squirearchy, the soup-strainer. A genuine specimen is now rare. It was invaluable in conferring at least a temporary impression of respectability and prudence even when these qualities were lacking. It was another marque which could not be worn without due care and attention. Contrary to the implications of its name, it was more hindrance than help when eating and drinking, and led to the redesign of table ware. Tea cups were made with a gridded section which kept the moustache out of harm's way while its owner refreshed himself. My grandfather had one.

Lack of the device was apt to lead a soup-strainer to lose its pristine gloss and symmetry, and to degenerate into the next best thing, the walrus. Much that was endearing attached to this mode, still sported today by bluff old brigadiers and the like. But in the golden age when moustaches were more than mere accidents of Nature, the walrus was held to indicate a moustache owner who had seen his best days. Its antonym was the tooth-brush. This satisfied humanity's ever-present craze for bantamization. So far from seeking to enhance their moustaches, its devotees behaved like ladies with chihuahuas, vying with each other to produce a smaller one.

Civilian Britain never had much use for wax. Not so the Army of yesteryear. Warrant officers laboured to produce projections like poignards on either side of the face, presumably in the belief that this would enhance their reputations for ferocity and prestige. A similar faith in waxed points pervaded the Balkans (the world's great forcing ground of moustache evolution) until a generation ago. Few reputable bandits or political agitators would have deigned to earn their daily bread unless so adorned.

My own contribution to our gross national moustache-product is unspectacular. It reflects my disposition – unobtrusive, neat but not gaudy. In this the evidence of those ancestral portraits suggests a genetic reversal. For they in the fine flowering and infinite variety of their natural embellishments, could not be so lightly dismissed.

FEBRUARY 1973

MESSRS VICE

OBSOLESCENCE RANKS HIGH among life's burdens. Its onset was brought home to me with diplomatic emphasis last winter. Now each summer Saturday brings poignant reminders. The news broke in a letter from my friend the secretary of the cricket club. That he had written a letter at all should have forewarned me. If he has anything to communicate he normally buttonholes me at an inconvenient moment and does the job verbally, to the detriment of my wordly cares; he himself appears to have none.

The epistle announced that the club, in annual general meeting assembled, had elected me a vice-president. So that the full significance of this should not be lost, it was added that the decision had been reached unanimously and (final ignominy) enthusiastically. There was more to come, for this was a missive, rare in village cricketing circles, extending to no fewer than two paragraphs.

The second, phrased with a tact so exquisite as to suggest some practice, introduced a financial consideration. Presumably to spare me doubt and embarrassment, it casually mentioned that other vice-presidents forked out a fiver a year each. It left me to draw for myself the comparison between this upper-crust figure and the annual sub of £1.05 which had latterly been my liability as one of the rank and file, it having been doubled with much else on decimalization. There remained the duty of writing to thank the club for the honour conferred on me, enclosing the cheque. The stiff upper lip still has its uses, so my realization of the true motivation was not alluded to. When all else has been withdrawn, one keeps one's pride.

I am man of the world enough to know the bitter truth which underlay the club's letter. In terms of principle it was official recognition of my decrepitude. In terms of practicality, it bade me abandon hope of ever again being in the team, however dire the crisis, however feeble the opposition, even as a non-bender. For me, it seemed, there was nothing left except the junior vice-president's deck chair (the one which merits its own insurance policy) and, when I have matured for a decade or so in my new rank, a Panama hat. A bleak prospect indeed, and one not shared by those more fortunately placed. The Boycotts of this world, if not picked for England, can always drop back on their counties. It is unthinkable that Yorkshire will ever have the brazen nerve to write to *him* announcing that he has been unanimously and enthusiastically elected a vice-president. Even if they did, other strata remain before he comes down to village cricket.

For us at the grass roots of the game, and that is about all there is to play on in a summer like this, a vice-presidency is the ultimate thumbs-down. Yet even in its afterglow cricket projects its ancient graces. When stumps are drawn, shadows lengthen, and a school is formed at the inn, no mere playing members are mannerless enough to usurp the priority of a vice-president in thumping the bar and calling for pints. In the countryside chaps still know their place; at appropriate moments it is right behind you.

The thought raises a question. Do vice-presidents know theirs? I suspect not. It would be presumptuous for a new recruit to the great vice-presidential brotherhood to tell the old stagers what to do. But unity is strength, and fair play for vice-presidents a crying need in a world where every interest has its pressure group.

When Saturdays bring the rattle of the gang-mower and the tapping-in of stumps, self-pity is countered by the realization that no man suffers alone. All round, unbeknown, are other vice-presidents of this and that, bearing their fate and meeting their liabilities with the dignity and fortitude which my ambition is to emulate. Most of us, thus branded as useless in all other roles, may share one other characteristic. How many men have actually asked to become vice-presidents, as distinct from merely being told they have metamorphosed as such, and will they kindly shoulder their packs and soldier on? Mighty few, I warrant. It must be the world's least-sought honour, other than the Irishman's rise. Far be it from me to claim to be sounding a first blast of the trumpet on their behalf. But this faint toot expresses fellow felling for a phalanx of solid citizenry whom the rest are accustomed to take, quite literally, for granted.

JUNE 1974

TURN OF THE SCREW

ONE SIMPLE MEASURE for the betterment of mankind would be the instant abolition of all labour-saving devices. The benefit would go well beyond the obvious one of securing full employment. Things could actually be done more quickly, more efficiently and with less frustration without them.

For temporary lack of a better implement, I have been using that abomination of the twentieth century, a ratchet screwdriver. It exemplifies all that is worst in what we know as progress. Consider its defects. Men with red blood in their veins and a modicum of intelligence can drive screws with no other aid than the non-automated kind. They are beautiful in their simplicity and lie sweetly in the hand. Many is the screw which I have thus cosseted home, apparently embedded for eternity.

They are tools for craftsmen of the old school, the kind of men with the trained dexterity to place the head of the blade in the notch of the screw and twist. But the busybodies, for motives on which I have my own theories, must needs invent something supposedly better but actually much inferior and unavoidably more expensive. The ratchet version is apparently designed for those incapable of doing more than push. Far from saving labour, this contraption means that the user must first ensure that it is in the right gear. If it is not, then it will unscrew instead of screwing; if it is, it will slip into the wrong gear as soon as progress is being made and, in pattern with most such developments, retrogression will result. If the user, maddened by such a happening, engages neutral (should he be able to find it) and seeks to proceed as if it were a screwdriver of yesteryear, the degree of disconnection, vibration, and general oscillation will greatly handicap his efforts.

One way or another, I suspect, women are at the bottom of this. Now that the majesty of the law has given them equal opportunities to drive screws, attempts have been made to cash in on feminine lack of confidence by adding complications and refinements to already functional instruments. Whatever the motive, this has failed. Except for my females of the species, a non-ratchet screwdriver would have been available for me. Three were missing from the work bench. The subsequent inquest revealed that one had been lifted by a daughter to lever illicit toffee out of a saucepan; another had been purloined by the other daughter to stir a pony mash; the third had come to roost for undisclosed reasons in my wife's handbag, she being a compulsive (and reasonably efficient) driver of screws into any penetrable surface at most hours of the day and night.

Technology resembles modern government. That which is intended is not achieved, but something eventuates which was neither contemplated nor desired. The world is full of apparatus which has made life worse instead of better – the telephone which corrupts good manners, the computer which multiplies bank errors, the electric razor which obviates soap and water, the power-driven carving knife which causes those who do not suffer from St Vitus's dance to produce results as if they did. The list is endless. We could all add to it. Let us look on the bright side instead.

Though they can be counted on the fingers of one hand, some innovations of my lifetime have made the world a better place. At the top of the list I would place the gum boot. Actually it is older than I am, but I can remember it as an innovation still struggling for recognition. Second to it is the plastic sack, for its innumerable secondary uses, as well as for its weatherproof (though not ratproof) qualities. Third, for me, come quilted jackets, in which to be cold or wet is impossible. But these are developments in materials, not of mechanics – the less of which we have, the better.

JUNE 1978

ORDER OF THE BATH

NOWHERE IS MAN more truly master of his environment than in the bath. There his merest whim can be translated into reality as the surrounding technology conforms to his wishes. If there be paradise on earth, this is it. To life, suffused in steam and caressed by fragrant water, is bliss itself. To be able to restore the fading warmth by turning the hot tap with one's big toe is a power of command not bestowed elsewhere. To watch the beaded bubbles congregating in the tail of the pool when one sits up is a pleasant adjunct to unwinding after effort.

Suppleness returns to stiffened muscles. Skin forgets the strictures of tight garters or the strap of a heavy game bag. Thus comforted, the inner man tactfully declares a readiness for dinner, coupled with the growing anticipation of a gin or two. All in all, the bath is a great place to be. I only wish it were possible to stay there longer. Unfortunately, equipped as it is, my household has not permitted this particular indulgence.

As Archimedes observed, the bath is apt to be the scene of displacement; if not of the water, then of the next would-be bather. Recognition of this has led me to express in the past, perhaps immoderately, my conviction that every head of household is entitled to his own bathroom. The deputy head of my household, while adroitly refraining from ambitions on her own behalf, has disastrously taken me at my word.

Armed with a steel tape, and with a local builder as her ally, she has established that certain nooks and crannies in the house are capable of conversion into shower-baths. One of them, regrettably, adjoins my dressing room. So, soon, lucky fellow that I am, I shall indeed have my own bathroom. But at the price of grievous deterioration in the quality of life. An ablutionary future in a cramped and antiseptic oblong, about as roomy as an upended coffin, does not please me. For shower-baths, unless cold, have no place in civilised living.

Instead of reclining, as a man is entitled to do after a day's toil or vigorous exercise, there will be those eel-like contortions under the spray which recall some esoteric Indian dance. My big toe will be as good as redundant. Control of that environment will be by the mixing valve, a notoriously unpredictable gadget whereby the bather is alternately scalded and frozen.

This may be all very well for the Finns, but for an Englishman it is a poor substitute for the pickling process which has become part of my life. It has been explained, of course, that my days of horizontal bathing are not totally ended. I shall still be welcome to the delights of full immersion. But think, she says, what a boon the shower-bath will be when two of us wish to use a bathroom at the same time.

There is no element of doubt about which of us will then be the unlucky contender. The propinquity of the shower-bath to my own domain gives me a walk-over for the short straw.

So I foresee a bleak existence in which the duty of showering will displace the enlargement of the spirit which is conferred by genuine bathing, along with the purification process. Instead of lying at ease, while meditations of cosmic scope grow in my mind, I shall find myself dressed and presentable half an hour too soon, with nothing to do but reflect upon the good old days. And good indeed they were, as countless numbers of my contemporaries will agree. The bath has left its mark on the British nation. One glance at a man's face tells me if he is a bather of the old school, a luxuriator, a devotee, almost a worshipper; or whether he is one of the in-and-out-in-five-minutes fraternity – clean enough, but not spiritually uplifted, so to speak.

The bath, I estimate, is a 30 per cent component of the complexion of those well-seasoned Britons whose cheerful and vigorous countenances stand out amid the pallor of the age. Their ruddy hue bespeaks a lifetime's devotion to fresh air, whisky, and hot water. I am faithful to this excellent design for living, in due moderation, and being careful to mix the last-named components only in exceptional circumstances. To maintain the same degree of fidelity will be difficult under the new arrangements. But I have not been churlish enough to veto them. The organisational advantages cannot be denied. I only hope that in my hours of envy she has the self-restraint not to sing.

DECEMBER 1978

ON SIGNING OFF

FASHIONS CHANGE, EVEN in valediction. Because the last words of an encounter remain uppermost in memory, those on parting have special importance. Some of them reflect the spirit of their age.

Farewell, in modern idiom, has an implication of finality not inherent in its purpose or in the Saxon syllables themselves. They mean no more than the increasingly used 'Safe journey' for which there is ample justification in this age of motor-cars and muggers. One of the most elegant of leave-takings, it fell out of common speech a century ago, retaining a literary usage.

Goodbye, contracted from 'God be with you,' was its contemporary and has, of course, survived. But it is raw material for adaptation. What has happened to Goodbye reflects the impulse to dismantle formality, generally by shortening. The absurd Bye-bye dates from the First World War. Its implications are juvenile, but its variations intriguing. It has become a symbol in verbal shorthand, meaning either more or less than it says.

'Bye-bye now,' with its overt suggestion that separation will be short-lived, generally presages no such thing. Often it is the dismissal signal for some telephonic bore. By adding the word 'now' the prospect is invited that the conversation's unfinished business will be resumed (coupled with an unspoken determination to the contrary).

'Bye . . .' in the singular, emitted a little breathlessly and with a Shakespearian dying fall, is strictly for feminine exploitation. It is uttered by ladies who consider their listener to be aware of their attractions (or if not, he ought to be), in the nicest possible way, of course. Experience has taught me how to deal with that one.

Other up-to-the-minute vogue phrases have come and gone in my lifetime. 'Chinchin,' with its undertone of Bertie Wooster, died out long since. The fatuous 'See you' survives for those who must have an alternative at all costs to the established term. 'So long', equating with '*au revoir*' and '*auf weidersehen*', evidently has its uses for some.

Of all the moderns 'Cheerio' alone commends itself to me, and then only in Scotland. There, spoken tunefully on a rising inflection, it conveys warm goodwill more readily transmitted by Celts than by the more reserved Saxons. The world momentarily seems a better place. These variations on the theme of how to part leave me wondering at the phenomenon of slang in general. Is it not simpler, in this instance, merely to say Goodbye? Then no doubt exists what is meant.

Some folk do, of course; and some folk do not. Even in my own family there are some of each. The dividing line between the two, and the reasons for it, both raise questions. Observation suggests that the acquisition of slang expressions, and resistance to them, are not governed solely by environment and company, as most parents assume them to be. Resistance, anyway, seems a matter of genetic accident. A brief progeny test supports the view.

Our household is not distinguished by formality of speech. But it is rich in case histories for analysing the acquisition of verbiage. Some contrasts speak for themselves. My own contribution is said to be mystifying to strangers in a manner familiar among those who have soldiered in foreign parts. The spoken word becomes fortified by service expressions, generally more colourful than those in civilian life, and by names and phrases infiltrated from other languages. My wife meets the ups and downs of domestic life with a repertoire of mild expletives of the 'Crumbs' and 'Hell's bells' variety.

As would reasonably be expected, one daughter seizes upon every new expression with the joy of a connoisseur, moulding it into her vocabulary as if anxious to become an anglicised Damon Runyon. Not so her younger sister. She, with maximum exposure to the sum of the idiosyncracies of the rest of us, maintains the unsullied conventions of Jane Austen's time. And, moreover, has always done so. Though bid 'Night, night' like millions of other small girls, her response was never other than a precisely enunciated 'Goodnight'. Now, as teenagers, when her sister acknowledges first meeting at the breakfast table with 'hallo' or any other variant, her own answer is an unselfconscious, wholly natural 'Good morning'.

Being able to remember their grandparents and some of their great-grandparents, I marvel at the way in which the microscopic links in the chain of life transmit details as small as these. My daughters' ancestry includes some who were uninhibited in speech or habit, and others who were prim. Their characteristics re-emerge in the new generation not fused or diluted but distinct.

DECEMBER 1980

STAGE COACH

SOME THINGS DO not change. The inside of a bus is one of them. Stepping aboard for the first time in 20 years or so was a return to old, unforgotten, comfortable things. Ill-chosen indeed were the words of the testy Oxford latinist:

> What is this that roareth thus,
> Can it be a motor-bus?
> Yes, the smell and hideous hum
> Indicat motorem bum.

These are mean, ungenerous comments on a respected institution. Though possessing its homely aroma, a bus can be condemned as malodorous only by crabbed spirits. That buses in general emit a degree of sound is generally admitted. But their sonorous pedal notes in no way qualify for the adjective hideous. Yet again, an academic mind failed to grasp normality.

Britain, especially rural Britain, would be impoverished without its buses. Not mainly, or even much, in the matter of transportation be it added, for buses seldom run when or in the direction required. It is as social adjuncts that they are irreplaceable. My long divorcement from buses reflects no loftiness in life-style, simply harsh necessity. Society has less infra-structure nowadays, so a man must do more for himself, driving himself instead of being driven in idle luxury by a bus-driver. Buses belong to a more spacious age than this, and those who ride in them must command more leisure than has been bestowed on me.

Five minutes here, five minutes there, while waiting for a bus to arrive, can seldom be spared. To be decanted ten minutes' walk from wherever one is bound is an interruption in that streamlining of time factors which modern life inflicts upon us all. Occasionally, say once in two decades, greater misfortune occurs to us whom modern pressures otherwise condemn to perpetual self-locomotion. In my case it was a flat battery in a car parked at the station while I was in London for the day. Darkness had fallen; garages were shut. Telephoning home for a rescue mission produced the wifely response that there was still a bus, instructions where to catch it, and an unspoken suggestion between the words that perhaps I might have thought of that for myself.

Well, perhaps I might. But buses do not leap readily to minds already pre-occupied with flat batteries. With some sense of unfamiliarity, I joined the queue. Reassurance returned when, one by one, we climbed the steps and paid our fares to, of all people, the driver. Another item had fallen out of the infra-structure. In my day buses had conductors. Otherwise, old familiarities revived. On the floor lay the decaying tickets and trampled matches of past journeys. Up front, ladies clutched handbags, observed, and talked in whispers. Astern, men took their seats and lit their pipes, enveloping in blue haze a courting couple self-conscious in a corner.

Only one seat was vacant. Natural selection had left it next to the most disastrous old bore for miles. No matter. Since I would have no chance to speak, there was no need to listen. An occasional sub-conscious exclamation kept my end up while the long-receded, youth-impregnated world of the bus re-created itself. Because it is a shared, communal thing a bus attracts affection. This grows into the charisma which surrounds other trusted forms of mass-mobility. Great ships with quadruple funnels and baritone sirens, the steam locomotives which hissed and chuffed through bygone years are among them. Beside them the honest, red-painted, meandering country buses of the lanes are worthy of their place, so essential to their neighbourhoods that the more learned of my colleagues write leading articles about them.

After ten minutes our bus stopped. The door opened itself, such being among the remote-control marvels of the age. Somebody got out, and in came the fresh evening air, bitter with the tang of straw-burning. It was a reminder. Though the bus comes and goes for all, it is a small world of its own, only intermittently renewing contact with the wider world outside. Glowing orange in the night, its dim internal light deepened by the condensation on its windows, it threads its way through fair weather and foul from village to village like a mobile club. In it confidentialities are made public which would otherwise be safe as in a confessional.

There is something about a bus which binds a man to his fellows. 'Saw you on the bus the other night,' said an eye-witness days later. He has been seeing me every day for years, but does not remark on my presence anywhere else. And news gets around, when it concerns the bus. 'Heard you were on the bus,' said somebody else. Socially, it seems, I have arrived; 15 years late of course, but better that than never.

But such fortification of self-esteem is a small thing beside the rediscovery of a crucible of human nature. From far away and long ago memories come flooding back of days when the bus was essential to the daily background. In its way, it was part of the turning seasons. From summer time, when the conductor would lever open the windows with a giant screw-driver to re-oxygenate the black-hole atmosphere within, to winter when those same windows were lashed by rain, the bus bound us together. In that amalgam of large-hipped men on small seats, dear old ladies saying Thank-you, macintoshes dripping, lethal umbrellas, parcels, the fumes of beer, snarling sheepdogs, babies crying, we had a concentrated dose of what normally happens at long range. To be in the thick of it again was a pleasure.

December 1980

FIGURING IT OUT

MY DAUGHTER, HAVING become a woman, has put away childish things. One of them, bequeathed to me, was her pocket calculator, by modern standards a modest aid to practitioners in mathematics. In its place she has been equipped (at paternal expense, of course) with a higher-powered and complex model more in keeping with O levels.

The transition to womanhood, which takes place unexpectedly in a few random hours in mid-teens, has many side-effects, not all predictable. Among those least expected is a sudden extension of parental horizons. The acquisition of a calculator split my world wide open. It put me on the same level as the pale, important-looking men who sit strumming their calculators in railway compartments, staring through heavy spectacles at columns of figures. This manner of whiling away a journey is beyond me, but my claim to parity makes me a fully qualified member of the modern human race, well and truly plugged-in to tomorrow's world.

Awareness of this produces a cosy feeling of the one-ness of mankind. No satisfaction, however, is totally complete. In this case misgiving enters with the memory (no disrespect intended) that Sir Harold Wilson publicly proclaimed that he used a slide rule to bolster up his arithmetic. A new light is thereby thrown on the concept of human unity. Either a calculator is in principle a kind of souped-up slide rule or (more likely since Sir H possessed one) a slide rule is akin to an up-market calculator. Do I really wish myself to be associated with forms of mental crutches which, in the case of the politician in question, cannot be disassociated from a degree of haplessness.

If Sir Alec Douglas-Home, cited because this is the stuff of history, could admit to doing his sums aided only by match sticks, was not his brain established thereby as demonstrably the more agile? Is not my place more properly beside him than among those whose natural faculty to add and subtract is in danger of atrophy through disuse? Each of us, of course, must decide this matter for himself.

I gave my calculator a trial run on Income Tax returns. Immediately this normally irksome process attained new rhythms. To the accompaniment of the little winking red light such totals as vehicle maintenance charges, fuel bills, telephone and electricity costs materialised obediently at finger-tip control. The process was interrupted occasionally when I totted up a column manually, so to speak, by way of a check. It was pleasing to confirm that the little device could compute as accurately as I can.

But a calculator soon proves just one more component of modern life which produces its own addiction. Soon one is calculating for calculation's sake. There are curious pleasures in assessing the cubic footage of the more regularly shaped rooms in the house, projecting the elapsation rate of the contents of the oil tank, comparing the urban and rural mpg's of the cars, and a host of other small conceits. Before these things can be done with any real degree of mastery, drills have to be practised. The designers of my machine had not placed their numerals 0 to 9 in the order long familiar to normal persons such as myself. Instead they adopted the sequence 7, 8, 9, 4, 5, 6, 1, 2, 3, 0. In time they will no doubt realise that in doing so they have made something of a gaffe, and become more systematic.

Meanwhile their hit-or-miss lay-out makes fingering the little knobs and buttons difficult. Sadly, to perform on the instrument with any sort of style or flair is as near impossible as makes no odds. I confess to a vision of myself as a master of the keyboard, an Arturo Rubinstein of the calculator. But that distinction seems unattainable. Part of the reason is my version's excessively modest size, little larger than a decently proportioned cheese biscuit. It is described a little drolly in its accompanying literature as a 'vest-pocket' calculator. Pockets in a vest would surely not be easily accessible, which may explain why I have never yet encountered pockets in any of the hundreds of vests which I have worn.

So there is small chance of my pummelling manfully away at the calculator, as would a maestro at a Steinway Grand. Instead I must be content to prod and twitch as if I were playing a miniature ukulele, to the detriment of the job satisfaction. Let us hope not only for more rational calculators in future, but also for some of them to be designed to a scale which will permit men to fulfil their aspirations through them. Small is not always beautiful.

Meanwhile the eternal contrast between ancient and modern remains. On the one hand I hold in my grasp the means to end the tyranny of figures. On the other my regard for the sanctity of established customs makes me aware of what has been lost as well as gained. To keep alive the obsolete crafts of our ancestors is a fetish of rural life. For once I shall indulge it and in the privacy of my study cast aside the crossword, roll back the march of Time, and recreate the lost pleasures of some honest British long division.

JUNE 1982

JOY WAGON

COME ON IN here. Don't quite know where you're going to sit. Let me take your gun. Terribly sorry; is it your foot or your dog I'm standing on? Good heavens, your lunch! Worse and worse. Never mind; we'll all shake down when we charge the hill.'

Thus we all are once again assembled here, and half-way through the first morning of another shooting season. Rain falls, of course. It always does, this year. The ratio of wet clothes to cubic footage makes the air inside like soup, thick soup. No matter. It is not possible to breathe anyway. We are too tight-packed to expand the ribs. But who worries about breathing in a Land-Rover, in England, in November?

Well I do, for one. Because I have just heard something from the rear of the vehicle. The rear of the vehicle is the bit from which one can see out backwards. 'Jump in here with us,' says an eager voice. 'Plenty of room! Now then shove up, somebody. Here's a space, next to me.'

No genius is needed to know that an enterprising fellow-traveller has clapped eyes on the bobbish wife of a walking gun who, being with the beaters, has left her unattended. A neighbour with iron hips gains eight inches at my expense. Apparently this is enough, though she must be wider than that.

'All aboard?' comes a voice from the flight deck forrard. This is the bit from which they should be able to see out forwards, but often cannot. We do not know it yet, but one limitation is that two girl stops are sitting on the bonnet. 'Giving a bit of bite to the front-wheel drive' comes over the air. It means nothing to us. Presumably the driver approved the view.

Visibility, like respiration, is a mere hand's breadth here in the cargo department. This is the distance which separates my face from the fangs of a black Labrador, grinning like a politician on polling day. The engine starts. The clutch engages. We move off. Our life-style, until then far from gracious, deteriorates further. Lurches spill the starboard passengers into the laps of those to port. We charge the hill. A hare, swinging from a game hook, enwraps my neck like a warm wet stole. 'Hang on, everybody,' comes a warning shout from up front, 'got to give it everything!'

Our small world heaves like a depth-charged submarine. The front wheels go one way, rear wheels the other. Then they spin. The engine roars. Blue smoke appears. Metal surfaces from all sides, and from below assail the person with varying consequences. The air, such as it is, is laden with stoicism and stiff upper lips. Two dogs start a grudge fight. Somebody says: 'Did you get up to the grouse this year, Reggie?' From below comes a succulent splashing. Mud squirts from under the tailboard, not all of it backwards. Land-Rovers can throw mud boomerang-fashion. It hurtles in on us. 'Good for the complexion,' is the rise-above-it verdict.

'You've got a chunk on the end of your nose,' says somebody else. 'Damn-all I can do about it,' responds bobbish wife's voice, 'I'm sitting on my hands.' No other soft seat is available. 'I'll get it off for you.' Squire of dames is now at full throttle. 'If I can reach my handkerchief.' Reach it he will, elbows working like pistons, even if the rest of us are maimed. We nearly all are, from another cause.

Brakes slam on. The vehicle halts. Bodies, guns, shooting sticks, lunches, flasks, dogs and pheasants from the previous drive cascade amid curses and the clash of metal. The human population shifts abruptly from rear to front. I feel the weight of my position in the community. In the general atmosphere of *sauve-qui-peut* even bobbish wife's nose is forgotten. 'Bloody sheep' floats back from the privileged ranks behind or alongside the steering wheel.

Cautiously the process of reorganization proceeds. Possessions are returned to their supposed owners. Limbs are rearranged in patterns less suggestive of all-in wrestling. Tail corn from the morning's pheasant round is shaken out of sleeves. Bobbish wife is asked if she is all right. We never know the answer.

'All out,' 'Guns this way,' bark the voices of those with leadership potential. Strong men grapple with the tailboard, weaker men spill out sideways, some walk feelingly in small circles like injured footballers as they ease away the pins-and-needles. 'You were going to tell me if you went up to the grouse this year, Reggie,' persists an inquirer who is not to be put off by trifles.

Normality is restored. Another journey has been survived. Life can go on again. A Land-Rover may not be, indeed, most certainly is not, the most comfortable of vehicles. But it arrives in its own idiosyncratic way, there is no limit to the number it can contain, and it has a rare knack of bringing everybody together.

NOVEMBER 1976

Moulds of Form

Ours is not a sartorially distinguished generation. Elegance is in temporary retreat. Nevertheless, a man spends 90 per cent of his time in clothes of one sort or another, and they come to reflect his attitude to life. This quintet touches upon five links between how we dress and how we act.

PRIDE OF TOPPERS

A WEDDING OVERHANGS us. To maintain morning coat, etc, as summer grazing for moth larvae seems a stagnant investment, so here I am in some quiet rooms in Central London where men discreet as family solicitors supervise the sartorial glory of those detailed for marriages, Ascot, the Garden Parties and occasions of comparable formality, in other words, the dress-hire department of you-know-who. Thus far all has gone well. My reflection stares back at me from a long mirror. We confront each other. The object is to assess the shape, fit and slope of a grey top-hat. A cousin looms up, preparing for the same great day.

'What are you putting that on for?' he asks ungrammatically. I tell him. 'Damn waste of money,' he responds. 'You won't wear it. No sooner put it on than you take it off again. Then you lose it. Never have one myself. If needed, soon find some other fellow's.'

Like that earlier and more famous wedding guest, his words leave me a sadder and a wiser man. Undoubtedly there is substance in his words. Yet they impose serious difficulties on those conscientiously resolved to do their duty by kith and kin. It would be unthinkable if base motives of cost and personal convenience precluded Our side from achieving parity in toppers with Theirs. Carried to extremes, total abstinence from toppers could leave our whole tribe bareheaded against the massed greys and lavenders of the opposition. I resolve that I shall do the right thing. I hire my topper as usual.

This emboldens me to put the point to my temporary technical adviser on wedding garments as we sign the lease. His discretion does not wilt. 'Indeed yes, sir,' he responds, folding my temporary trousers with careless ease into a knife-edge crease, 'quite a number of gentlemen prefer not to take a hat nowadays. I think they find it a nuisance, sir.' Reassurance that the hatless still rank as gentlemen does not tempt me to join their number. If a topper constitutes my responsibility you won't catch me laying it down. Won't you, though? Picture what happens.

In the sunlit lane outside the lych gate one unfolds from the car and dons the topper. Instantly femininity hems one in. Charm . . . gaiety . . . recognition . . . in less time than a sprinter needs to win an Olympic Gold, off comes the topper. It is long odds that it will ever go on again, at least until another wedding comes round. Its only useful function now is a receptacle for gloves. Here my sympathies are with those who go on record as recognizing the nuisance-potential of toppers. Placed under the pew seat it may or may not stay *in situ*. If it does it may well be trampled, dented or in other ways defaced.

If it doesn't (and it won't unless the pew backs join the floor) it may be heeled like a Rugby ball two or three rows to the rear. The leanings, turnings, peerings and general restiveness of a wedding congregation mean that feet are never still. Out of sight is out of mind, especially for a topper. Hence the ruthless common sense of my radical-minded cousin. If a topper is needed, as it will be, for a photograph or to wave amid the confetti showers as the happy couple drive away, there will be plenty around. Abandoned by the festive throng, pride of possession is short-lived.

Hence, too, that sad last duty of the ushers. As the shadows lengthen, and the first slammings of car doors begin their curfew on the day, these personable young men will make their final official appearance. Each with an armful of toppers, they will go the rounds striving to reunite the jetsam of the occasion with the respective owners and tenants. Only the owners will be interested. And I bet there will not be many of them.

SEPTEMBER 1972

ON SHINING FOOT

IF MY GRANDFATHER ever washed and dried a cup and saucer the circumstances must have been of unimaginable urgency and are unrecorded. However strong the evidence, I would go to my grave doubting that such a thing ever happened. A yeoman of England, he knew his limits. They stopped short of involvement in domestic activities. Even less tenable would be the proposition that he had ever cleaned his own boots. At the idea that he should clean not merely his own, but those of his spouse and offspring, the mind boggles. And for the further concept that this should be no emergency measure but a regularly established habit, the verb to boggle would understate.

No envy motivates my recording this. On the contrary, I take pleasure in an enjoyable experience available to me but unknown to him. In that haven which is the boot- and shoe-cleaner's world, a man is at peace as nowhere else, liberal thoughts fructify, and the mind may be enriched. In modern conditions of instant communication the nature of the task has its own rewards. Solitude is guaranteed. The telephone is out of earshot. To clean leather while watching television is impossible. Interruption and irritation being thus cauterized, preparations follow a drill.

First, to fix the date and time. These, narrowly variable, are decided after analysis of the radio programmes. Few human activities can coincide with symphonic music without detriment to either. This one can. The swish of bristles does not offend the music of the masters; but the music of some masters stimulates as does nothing else the swish of bristles.

Secondly, to deploy the stores required. Clean newspaper covers the table-top (tonight it was *The Times*, the advertisements for escort agencies making interesting reading, even though upside down). Polish, cloths and brushes are laid out in established sequence. The transistor is tuned.

Finally, to assess the customers, ranged by their proprietors in response to a declaration of intent. Fifteen or 16 pairs, masculine and feminine, fit fairly neatly into a symphony by Beethoven, Brahms or Tchaikovsky. In the next rank are Mozart, Haydn and Schumann, who inspire less effective rhythms. Schubert is useless as an accompanist for shoe-polishing, but for me he is small loss. Sadder to say, Sibelius and Dvorak also decelerate a proper shine.

Thus stimulated, a man may take pride in his work. Being a Gunner, I am not among those weaklings who use one brush to put on the polish and another to shine up. Successive batmen dilated upon the discipline of using one brush for both. The polish must then be used economically and accurately. If not, the brush becomes saturated and the desired gleam long in coming. Not for ease my prayer shall be. The job is done the proper way, even if it is thereby made a little harder.

So, in the still of the night and free of human intervention, the soaring strains give nobility to what some would think a mundane activity. The Sherlock Holmes, latent in every man, has a chance to make deductions. Junior daughter has taken to dribbling stones *en route* to school. Perhaps Freudian impulses lurk. She shall be watched. Whatever is it that women do to shoes when they go shopping? The lady of the house would seem more likely to have played football. Pair after pair come up for treatment. Rejuvenated, they go their way. The shortening line of the travel-weary, the lengthening line of those restored to health, combine to tell the story of patriarchal life in the neo-Elizabethan age.

With all accomplished, the fruits of my labour give me a sense of rectitude which in this respect even my grandfather did not know. Nothing like leather, they say. How true this is in the reflection of work well done. The sharp sparkle of black, the softer glow of ox-blood send a contented man to the decanter. And when the family parade, in detail or as a unit, my eye falls by habit to their feet. Smug as it is to say so, then is my reward. I have seen sunshine flash from a battery of swinging boots. It looked good at the time. My own toil looks even better.

JUNE 1973

NETHER GARMENTS

NO MAN CAN be wholly indifferent to his trousers. One particular aspect of our nether garments has been engaging my attention. It stems from the profundities of science. Whether one stands or sits when donning them or taking them off is of much consequence. Far from being an idle observation or just a personal habit, whichever one does is said by doctors to indicate one's defiance of Time. So long as we can remain standing, I read, we are keeping the grim reaper at bay. Those of us who sit are not the men we were. In earlier times the matter would have been of actual or potential concern to a mere 50 per cent of the population.

Now that ladies as well as men regard trousers as normal wear, the figure increases to 100 per cent, so the public interest becomes overwhelming. It remains to develop the theme.

At the age of about 45 a man comes to accept that his youth cannot bloom for ever. Having left that milestone behind me, I have since become engrossed with the extent to which middle age can be prolonged. The time will come when senescence can no longer be denied, and a major interest will be in avoiding its consequences. Throughout this process I and the millions of other inhabitants of temperate climes will, several times a day, have been putting on and changing trousers. This mundane operation separates the men from the boys; even the old men from the old boys. As the senses decline towards write-off point, that of balance is one of the first to go. The young and lissom step nimbly from one pair to the next. Crabbed age finds a chair or (so it is reported) leans against a wall for support.

Of course there are extraneous circumstances, some of them dietary, adverse to equilibrium. Even so, those who find themselves careened to port or starboard cannot be oblivious to their position. I knew a most distinguished hunting man who lost for a whole season the capacity to remain upright. The reason was nothing more rash than a leap from bed at Reveille to switch on the radio and hear the Test scores from Australia. In his haste he ruptured those vital components near the ear which prevent a man from keeling over.

When we come to review our personal performances in this widely shared experience, as many of my readers will doubtless now do, it is fair to make allowances for extenuating circumstances. To assume some of the easier *marques* of trouser, such as pyjamas or plus-fours, should be well within the compass of any octogenarian. There are more advanced tests. Sternest of all for me is a certain pair of flatteringly close-fitting jodhpurs. The moment of truth comes when the heel has to go through the knee-section. This demands the flexion of a ballet dancer, the stability of a Cumberland wrestler, the patience of Job and, if all does not go well, much stamina. Truth compels admission that I would not undertake this feat if not within anti-toppling range of my dressing room table.

Breast-waders are less easy than they look. Fishermen intending to show off should step well back from the river bank. Were I young enough still to wear mess kit I should approach my overalls with caution. I cannot vouch for my manner of quitting them, the recollections of which are sometimes hazy.

Waterproof over-trousers should be excluded from assessment. Little difficulty is presented by getting into them, since they are dry and disciplined at the start of the day. At the end, when wet and mutinous, they stick like adhesive plaster, and to get out of them is akin to skinning oneself.

Such exceptions apart, the average trouser has not bested me yet. It presents a challenge which it is my intention to accept as long as I am able. But my gratitude to the medical men who have revealed this great truth is qualified. I am not sure that I shall welcome the inescapable inference when (I trust only at long last) I overbalance or subside into a chair.

JANUARY 1974

SONG OF A SHIRT

SOMETHING SITUATED ABOUT my collarbone riveted the gaze of a younger friend. 'What's wrong with your shirt?' he asked. Nothing to my knowledge being wrong with my shirt, I asked the symptoms. 'It looks like sweet itch to me,' came the reply. Truth dawned. To one of callow years a darned shirt is ground for amazement. It was the generation gap.

'Darned!' he repeated, as if to reassure himself that the word existed. 'If mine need darning, I buy another.' Of course he does. Likewise the rest of his age group. Hence the cost of living, the consumer society, and the disposable society. They may live long enough to learn differently.

When wear and tear afflicts my shirts, as happens where the points of a stiff collar abrade the linen, it seems natural that deft fingers should repair the damage. Inevitably there are visible signs of such handiwork. Any resemblance to sweet itch is incidental and I see no cause for embarrassment. On the contrary, these small accumulations of cross-stitching serve as a badge of rank. They are worn by those with the sense to make the most of their assets (and, one hopes, the assets of the world in general). It is time for all of us who wear darned shirts to stand up and be counted, and to declare ourselves separate from those profligate fellows who, every want provided in an age of unparalleled easy living, commit such social crimes as cutting string instead of unknotting it.

Extravagance does not stop there. Last week an otherwise agreeable young man actually threw away a neat little tobacco tin of exactly the right size to contain beeswax. We retrieved it from the waste-paper basket in his room and it awaits redeployment. Hours later, beside the river, he had borrowed my beeswax. Not for him to be reminded by the sight of a suitable container that he had no beeswax of his own, and hence to get some. If the Lord will not provide, somebody else will; such is the young set's principle. Self-reliance is for those of riper years. It was not ever thus in our less cushioned lives.

Soldiers do not cut string. Should the unimaginable happen, and some rookie absentmindedly attempt to do so, goodbye to his hopes of promotion. Former soldiers do not burn baler twine. Miles of it are looped over a beam in our barn. One day I hope to discover what former soldiers should do with it. But destroy it . . . not likely.

As a boy I remember my grandfather, a man of substance, picking up a rusty pin, cleaning it, and parking it in the reverse of a lapel. 'We'll have that,' he said, 'it's metal.' Metal is one of the world's boons. It is not inexhaustible. Quite right that a man should be grateful for it, even reverent of it; that he should save it, however small the quantity, not throw it away.

Humanity now exploits recklessly, using up the assets of our planet, expending without re-creating. Only Nature can re-create. The process occupies millennia, and humanity is preventing it even starting. Suck dry, melt out, use up the useful elements in the earth. Then throw away all that is not dust. Preservation is an outmoded concept, widely dismissed now as a fetish of our ancestors but out of place today in a society in which most men think they know all. The wisdom of the East is not far behind what the oil sheikhs have done.

After only three decades, the spendthrift society makes accelerating inroads on the world's resources. It began, of course, in that most spectacular of all wastages, war. For me, contrast identified the change in thinking.

On leave, I had stayed with a civilian host who even at that time commanded six dozen shirts in routine use. As I then possessed three, it seemed to me that his margin for emergencies, totalling 69, was more than ample. Nevertheless, should wear occur, his casualties were darned to reduce risk of being caught short.

A few weeks later, my jeep paralyzed by a mortar bomb, I was towed into an American MT park and sought help. 'Try this buddy,' invited an ally. A new jeep was driven out. In it I drove away. I had not even signed for it. On my way rejoicing, the last scene shifted. Three robust GIs strained and heaved at my former vehicle. They were tipping it into a ravine. Our Army would have repaired it in those days. The old habit dies hard, even if only in shirts.

MAY 1975

CLAD IN MEMORIES

MY HAND, THRUSTING for a car-key, carried away the pocket lining, tore a hole in the tweed itself and emerged in the open air. A sorry sight indeed and one that carried an inevitable message. That faithful old jacket would be worn no more. A daughter, the only eye-witness, summed it up with feminine heartlessness. 'Mummy will be pleased, anyway,' she declared, as one who looked on the bright side. 'You can't stop her throwing it out now.' No, indeed.

The supposedly gentler sex do not share the masculine regard for senescent material objects. For us they do more than fulfil their function be it gun, golf club, collar stud or tweed jacket. They mark the passing ages of a man's life. Remembering the cubhunting meet at which it first came between me and the weather, recalling the newly-appointed Master whom it was thought seemly to impress by my latest sartorial acquisition, I realised that the old jacket had served me for 23 years. Ours had been an eventful, happy partnership. Hence my efforts to preserve it as something more than an earnest of days gone by.

During its near quarter-of-a-century it had withstood enough English weather almost to have become part of it. Sunshine had faded it, dimming its check. Rain had soaked into it, sapping its fibre. But sapping it only slowly, because rain had been its material's native element. Before my time, it had clad some Cheviot sheep. Yet the old jacket never conceded to time the style it had carried through all the changing scenes of life since the days of the second Macmillan government. Seconds before my extrusive fist burst it asunder, the old tailor who cut and fitted it could still have felt pride in his handiwork. By that thought the old jacket was fulfilling its function as a reminder of life's lessons.

The significance was that he had been an old tailor, and not a young one, who produced a garment capable of generating affection as well as of long service; so old, indeed, that he will be with his ancestors now. His memory lives on in my mind as demonstrating that though man learns by varied means, he improves not with knowledge but by experience.

For the best advice or service, wisdom dictates an elderly practitioner. The longer the tally of failures on which a man can look back, the greater his chance of avoiding them in what future remains. Spare me, therefore, young tailors, young lawyers, young doctors, young accountants; give me instead veterans of these professions. They can remember which mistaken ploys condemned earlier clients to looking like scarecrows, to wasting their substance, to graves or bankruptcy.

My old tailor had done well. His jacket sat neatly upon my shoulders, despite one being an inch-and-a-half lower than the other since striking mother earth all too sharply long since. It did not gape in a vulgar manner when I turned my head to look backward, a feat now beyond me – a limitation which life imposes on those who, in the modern phrase, stick their necks out. The relationship between me and my jacket became easy and companionable. In those faraway days it gave me confidence, not always otherwise felt, of being just right for the occasions on which I chose to wear it. These were varied and their character altered as its service lengthened.

In its flush of youth, its pattern still sharp and intimidating, I wore it when judging some hunter trials, which shows the esteem in which it was held. Not every hacking jacket looks at ease in association with a bowler hat, *de rigeur* on such occasions. But this one did. Moreover its selection was approved at connubial level. After a decade or so, such approval could no longer be taken for granted. The cool, appraising glance from across the breakfast table was apt to be followed by, 'Not that one again, surely', degenerating, as the 1970s ripened, into 'Oh, no, really!' when it was known that eyes other than ours would fall on me thus arrayed.

Signs that the shades were lengthening became irrefutable as we set off to take our children to a circus. There was a tell-tale hush as I prepared to start the car, then signs of nudging in the passenger seats, undeniable whispering and the family went on strike. Only when a substitute jacket had been brought did the expedition proceed.

So the ageing jacket became re-classified for private enjoyment only. At first it was donned for fishing and for walking round with a gun in counter-measures against woodpigeons and rabbits. More rain and more sun soaked into it. It was not the jacket it once had been, though in my opinion none the worse for that. For me, it still seemed to have a long future. Gardening and dog exercise make their special demands on the wardrobe. It is easy to overdress for either, but both justify some indications of bygone couth which I thought the old jacket represented rather well until my hand appeared – not through the sleeve but through its self-created aperture.

What then? My reference to a jumble sale aroused laughter. White tie and tails seem to be expected by jumble-sale patrons nowadays. Scarecrow? Guy Fawkes? No such indignity could be tolerated. An end, discreet though humiliating, was decreed via the dustbin. Thus the moment of parting has come. All that remains is for me to hand it over. Looked at dispassionately in a bleak morning light, its decrepitude is obvious. The best thing about it is the one remaining leather button and even that is damaged.

With the knife that so often lay in the old jacket's pocket, I cut off the button and put it into a drawer with sundry treasures. It is much misshapen and scarred by the milk teeth of a fox terrier. She went to ground for the last time 8 years ago, aged 15.

MARCH 1982

The Echoing Trumpet

Once a man has been a soldier, the tincture never leaves him. It is always there, ready to respond to the touch of memory, illuminating by its contrast his remaining days of peace. Soldiering is for young men whose minds, still fresh and uncrowded, absorb its many impressions in all the vividness of youth. When the trumpet echoes down the years its message is not one of hardship and destruction, of which men do not need reminding, but of comradeship, high spirits, and the strange fascination of the very ordinary material objects which loomed large in the stark scene of past campaigns.

SOLDIERS' CHORUS

IT WAS HARDLY a song without words; better indeed had it been so. The subject-matter concerned the subsequent experiences of one who had been sitting by Reilly's fire, eating chips and drinking porter. No good purpose would be served by quoting further. It will be familiar to all soldiery, past and present of all ranks, who have ever been within earshot of a sergeants' mess party. This means all of them, there being no limits to the audibility of sergeants' mess parties.

Whether it is equally familiar to the Royal Navy and the Royal Air Force is not known to me. We of the Army are inclined, in our modest way, to assume that the other armed Services are more refined or less robust or both. It is difficult to imagine such polite-sounding personages as engine room artificers and leading aircraftmen bawling forth in alcoholic fervour the lusty runes of a pongo. The rune in question is mentioned here for the magnificance of the air to which it is sung. This combines tonal vigour with a musical inspiration comparable to its counterparts in *Faust* and *Trovatore*, and which some might think misplaced if they knew the lyric. Hearing the uplifting chorus afar off when arriving suitably late at an old comrades' supper, I confess to fearing what the neighbours might think. With relief I discovered that the organizers had shown the good sense to site the event at an erstwhile carters' inn a mile from the nearest habitation in any direction.

This tactical remoteness ended all inhibitions on indulgence in martial melodies. The Great Wheel was rendered with timely *diminuendo*. This also is a ballad unlikely to be sung by bishops, and it is a piquant thought that some of their Lordships may remember it from campaigning days. With throats well flushed with ale we passed on to Mobile, Deolali Sahib, the Little Harness Room across the Square, that dirge-like valediction now delicately watered down to Bless 'em all, and Thora Pani, Thora Char. These were songs which resounded through countless campaigns. They are an elemental corporate voice of those who won all the battle honours of the British Army, of all the regiments of the living and the dead. Colours laid by in great cathedrals once flew among these rhythmic crudities to which fighting men give tongue, shocking through the thought may be to those who were never lonely, weary and imperilled far away with only basic memories to fire their muse.

They are the songs of heroes and cowards, of those on their way to greatness and those heading for perdition. They have echoed, to our knowledge, amid the mud of Flanders, desert sands, and in firefly-studded eastern nights. Where else? And for how long? The words, some of which would make a pornographer blench, have a modern or a timeless ring, according to viewpoint. If Shakespeare was right in his fictional reconstruction of camp-fire talk at Agincourt, soldiers' idioms have not changed much in 500 years. Perhaps soldiers' music is a lasting heritage too.

That dedicated campaigner, Field-Marshal Lord Wavell, referred disparagingly in *Other Men's Flowers* to the folk songs of British troops. Here, for once, his appreciation seems open to question, especially if drinking songs are included. Any soldier whose knees are brown reckons to spend as much time drinking as marching and with pot in hand his spirit is set free.

If nobody is collecting the war songs of the British, somebody should start now. They are part of history. Their musical derivation is worth scholarship. Subtract those of evident camp-concert origin, generally based on hymn tunes or parodies, and there remain some which, unrecorded otherwise, must have been passed down by generation after generation of fighting men. They may well come from far away and long ago, from once-stricken fields which now seem but names in textbooks and yet, unrealized by us, are living memories. The songs of crusaders and troubadours, not all saintly in their day, may be in the pedigree of those we sang in the lamp-lit, malt-fragrant Shades behind the carters' inn while frost rimed the hedges under a starry sky. Ancient or modern, it was good to call again the tunes of the valorous if sometimes bawdy trade of soldiering.

APRIL 1973

SERENADING THE MULE

A GHILLIE RECOGNIZED my fishing bag, and we had a quick and extra dram. It baffles most people. This is not the haversack in which I carry tactical necessities on the river, but the larger compendium which stays in the car as the quartermaster's store of my fishing life. Some such reticule was doubtless meant when that dean of fishing bores, Izaak Walton, quacked: 'Boy, bring me my dubbing bag.'

Mine contains not merely fly-tying material. There are also apt to be assortments of reels, lines, gaff-heads, spools of nylon, hooks, tools, books, bottles, ancient chunks of beeswax, shot, spoons, floats, obsolete licences, letters from friends and, as I recently discovered, the piece of cheese which I intended to distribute to the chaffinches on the Wye several years ago but never got round to handing over. Since none of these items is visible externally, why should people look strangely at my fishing bag? Its appearance is distinctive. It is made of rawhide. It is shaped somewhat like a small coffin. It has stalwart iron fittings and straps of particular design. These, with an odour a quarter of a century old, are the give-away. Yet only occasionally does some bystander know that he is looking at a yakdan and turn his thoughts to mules.

Men who do so come of a race apart, distinctive in age-group and appearance. They are lean, their thin faces seamed and wrinkled by hot sunshine, and even more by hot winds long ago. The yakdan was, still is, the universal holdall of those who travel the high and arid Asian mountains with mules as companions and friends. And that odour? It combines the perfumes of Arabia, and of Persia and old India, too. Nor are these the artful distillations of the seraglio, but the elemental smells of lonely places east of Suez, and that is a man's world.

From where I sit the air brings in through the open window the rosiness of an English summer. But as it eddies over the top of the bookcase, my yakdan's parking place, it surrenders to the indestructible orient's smell of old times and brings to me deathless memories. That leather absorbed and is for ever giving back the sunset tang of burning dung, strong curry, griddled atta, mule sweat, man sweat, baked dust, camel harness, tamarisk and dry thorns. Shelley said that the champak odours fall like sweet thoughts in a dream. Let them go. My yakdan is good enough for me with its reminder of long days with the mule trains coughing in the dust.

Companions and friends, I wrote earlier. It is no use being a mule's companion without also being his friend. You get nowhere if you try. A mule can sum up a man as a soldier does, both pitilessly and generously. The mule is an old soldier at heart. Let him down, laugh at him or be soft with him and you've had it, as the saying is. Be fair to him (he knows his rights as well as any barrackroom lawyer) and he does not fail his duty.

His duty? Or hers? Does it matter? It is all the same to a mule. And here, perhaps, is the clue to the singular completeness of mule character. Mules are finished articles and not, as we are, merely stages in a process of genetic change which, with each of us as a tiny stepping-stone of progress, will one day produce a superior race of men. Every mule, by contrast, is the end of his particular line of development. With no contribution to make to posterity, a mule exists only for the present. All the qualities of every ancestor come to a head, and to a full stop, in each mule.

Long-eared, long-faced, long-memoried and long of teeth (which can meet in the anatomy of a passer-by at surprising distances when these characteristics coincide), quick of heel, disciplined, bolshy, laconic, tough and independent, mules fit naturally into an army. They keep their end up. They thrive in an ambience of four-letter words, and quickly learn their significance. They become, grudgingly as in all things, the natural counterparts of the p.b.i.

Few modern, technological soldiers are likely to meet them. I'm glad I did. They taught me much. No man who has ever fumbled his efforts to put a pack saddle on a critical, experienced, long-service army mule which possibly has a hangover will ever again tackle an unfamiliar task without learning the proper way first. Sometimes I stand by my yakdan, close my eyes, inhale the message-laden scent of its leather and lose all thoughts of fishing. Smell, that most evocative of the senses, starts the others going – the feel of a soft nose butting me in the back, the taste of salt trickling into my mouth, the sight of loads swaying on an uphill trail, the sound of bhoosa being munched at the end of the day. If the Indian Army ever wonder why they did not get their yakdan back, they know now.

July 1972

A THANKSGIVING

NOBODY CAN JUSTLY accuse me of being a heavy drinker of water. But from time to time I take a glass, and when this happens it is generally the occasion for a small private ceremony. Those who have learned the value of water the hard way will understand.

I hold the glass up to the light and enjoy the knowledge that it is actually there, that it is clear and cold, and that it is all for me to drink, at one draught if I wish. I thank God for the major blessing of its presence in my hand, and for the minor ones of its translucence in contrast to some of the murky samples which have come my way, and of its freedom from the taste of chlorine. As I swallow it memories form a backcloth to what some may consider an uninspiring celebration. Those who can think thus of water may count themselves lucky, though probably few actually do so because men are slow to learn from the experience of others. I think again of days when the concept of fresh water in limitless quantities was wholly unattainable and almost unendurable, so constituting a mental torture additional to physical suffering; days when one army bottleful of brownish liquid, often containing small dead fish, hot by day, malodorous by night, and as nauseating as it was obsessive had to last 48 hours and sometimes 72; days when the big decision was not whether one could afford to take more than one mouthful, but whether that mouthful could actually be swallowed or should be spat back into the bottle to be savoured again later, beastly though it was.

We who shared such interludes know as something more than mere theory that water is the Creator's lifeline to the human race. With water we could hope to live to eat the next meal, however long it might be delayed. With food, but without water, expectation of life could be calculated in hours, and there would not be much likelihood of major error.

It is no surprise to me that Moses made so deep an impression on his people when, in their hour of crisis, he smote upon the rock. I once saw a similar feat performed, with results equally far reaching for 150 comrades, by a bombardier in Burma. With his axe, pick, general service, he smote upon the dessicated shale. The little hole he made filled within half an hour with a six-inch depth of water. Not much but enough for men who, like Coleridge's seafarers, had gone a night and a day with 'throats unslaked and black lips baked'. When I asked why he had done what he did at that particular spot, he recalled something he had learned as a Boy Scout and added that he had since become a water diviner. To us he seemed, and indeed was, the agent of Almighty providence. In a place where no sapling grew for many miles he could not exercise his art but had acted from forgotten knowledge, and a half-blind faith. Who shall say that a greater power had not provided the spark which exploded his weary thinking into action.

When the chance came later, I made sure he taught me divining. The term is well chosen. I found the feat within my power, and have since employed it usefully. That I, or anybody else, can find water through the uncontrollable twisting of living wood in passive hands no longer seems remarkable to me. No such gift is bestowed upon us for the discovery of anything else than water. But there is nothing else which we cannot, in the last accounting, do without.

Soon the harvest weather must finally give way to the equinoctial gales, and wet storms from the West. I shall bear with limited patience people complaining that 'it' is raining. Let the rains come. And let us, for a change, be grateful for what we are about to receive, and which we waste so profligately. When the rains sweep across the countryside, drumming through starless nights, bouncing off the gutters, splashing into water butts, flowing milkily in runnels from the chalk, or chocolate brown from blocked field drains in loam and clay, raising river-voices from trickles to gurgles and then to roaring floods, we shall be hearing and seeing the Almighty's elemental gift to all life here below. I for one shall lift up my heart.

SEPTEMBER 1972

MAN AND BOOT

LITTLE LESS THAN love links a man with his boots. The very word opens up horizons of endeavour and achievement. Mention boots and visions grow. The virile monosyllable strikes different chords from the grey and insipid nouns designating other footwear.

Looking back across the vista of the years, memories of my various boots leave me thankful for good times, hard times, and good friends in whose company they were worn. Looking forward across the unexpended portion of the same vista, the boots I have yet to wear summarize ambitions for the future. More mountains to climb, more horses to ride, more rivers to wade. The prospect puts me under starter's orders for a race with that old fugitive Time to do it all before too late. Win or lose, boots already have me in their debt. From slippered ease I salute them. They have helped me through days of gold and iron.

Far away now is the portentous day when first my legs slid into hunting boots. In the shop, surrounded by silver-haired men with the prestige of Harley Street surgeons, it had seemed improbable that instep and ankle could take the tight turn leading into the foot. But they did. The silver-haired men knew their craft. In the saddle afterwards there had been that unbelievable thing, the instant marriage of leather to leather. Boot and flap had come together and stayed together as if by magnetic force. My thanks have gone out for this reassuring union on many a cold morning when a horse had his back up.

My fishing boots now hang upside-down. Stuffed with newspaper, they are a habitation for earwigs, and heralds of the new season. Last year the grey Usk eddied and bubbled round their tops. Where next? Already salmon are in the early rivers of Ireland and Scotland. Before the glens are warm my waders will again have felt the tug of new waters.

Shooting boots are not what they were. To write this both grieves and pleases me. The thoroughbred leather version, worn below well-scrubbed spats, has gone out of my life. In there place has come rubber. The transition has not been without misgiving. Sometimes, pulling on the bland, green, comfortable, watertight, insulated, inexpensive newcomers, I wonder if I should resign from my club. To wear anything which does not require neatsfoot oil and dubbin negates a ritual of the shooter's life. Rehabilitation of boots formerly ranked second only to the cleaning of guns. Now they are merely held under a tap. This does not seem right. I can well use the time thus saved, but to me that which comes easily is suspect.

Many of us wore boots when nothing came easily. To a soldier it seems strange that the largest and most flamboyant boots of the Second World War were worn by airmen. They fought seated. My boots, officer's, marching, gave up the ghost while I was yet hale and hearty. Thereafter it was boots, ammunition, for me. I and my first pair reached the end of our tether together. The road leading from disaster repeated itself for weeks on end. Endlessly it led up into the invisibility of cloud; endlessly it led down into the invisibility of mist. The enemy had broken contact. There was no view in Asia to challenge that of one's own feet. To see them involved no loss of energy in lifting one's head. Endlessly one foot replaced the other, squirting up the khaki dust so that we seemed to march through knee-high smoke. Endlessly the uppers opened and closed on the protruding nails of the soles, like the jaws of two faintly snapping crocodiles. I had other pairs for the march back. They never won my heart as did the old wrecks which brought me out.

In these better times moments still come which are not very different. Down to a valley road after a climb, boots come off and shoes go on for the walk back to the hotel. Not for me alone, perhaps, that flash of communion with the tricorns on which our lives depend. Smoothed and polished by duty and endurance, they earn a glance of gratitude before they are stowed in the pack.

Boots have a voice, too, in urgency or ease. The rhythmic manly multiplied beat of those same ammunition boots comes to hard-pressed men as the sound of hope fulfilled when another company moves in. The crunch of boots on gravel, with an undertone of soft Highland talk as ghillies gather outside a rod room, is the best of overtures to a Scottish day.

Let the angels write me as a man of boots. There are many such, and we are a distinctive community when compared with those less solidly shod. For us the pleasant rigours, for them the dexterities of life. Providence gave me neither skill at games, nor interest in them, except to find an alibi for not playing them. But should all alibi fail I would parade with the cricketers, footballers and boxers, booted as they are, rather than with the golfers, tennis players and bowlers who tread their primrose paths in shoes.

JANUARY 1974

UNDER CANVAS

WRITE ME AS a man of tents. Before life passed half-time, and femininity conferred the silken touch, houses were the exception. A canvas spread, not a roof, was shelter from storm and sun. Brailings, not windows, admitted air fragrant of breathing earth and aromatic grass heads. Returning to soft life in solid buildings, the shutting of the door on the outer world was the knell for a lost freedom. Occasionally, reminders come to a heart long lost to Kedah.

My village carnival duties include sovereignty over the marquees. It is a position of responsibility without power. As in all things in all villages, a committee spirit supervenes. A plan has been drawn up. It had been debated and adjusted with vehemence and prolixity for months. Finally it was settled, and a fair copy drawn by the art master at a nearby school. All know that what he drew is no final solution but a basis for last-ditch negotiation.

On the appointed evening the stalwarts of the village assemble and, as is customary, take their shirts off. With every torso bared to the westering sun, the traditional question is put: 'Have we really got the beer tent in the right place, what with that business last year and all?' The answer will be reached quicker without me. The best course is to fade away and sort out trestles and muse upon the tents in pupal form, lashed up and dumped around. They recall the tents of a lifetime.

None, when cursing and grunting and heaving upon guy-ropes has resurrected it, will resemble the tent which sheltered me from Briasco Bridge to Jessami (a long way across Asia). That strip of tarpaulin, seven feet by four, raises the question: When does debris become a tent? The answer is: When it is somebody's home. Let none stigmatize my strip of tarpaulin as less than fit abode for an officer and gentleman. Though modest in proportions, and split at one end, it was commodious compared with some structures occupied by brothers-in-arms. Not for long did my thoughts turn back regretfully to the tent, officer's, 40-pounder, nationalized by the Japanese in the name of the Emperor, which it had replaced. This had afforded little space for social activities. It merely marked its occupant of some consequence. And nowhere was personal grandeur more wholeheartedly disclaimed than in the Don't-look-now-we're-being-watched war in Burma.

Later, promotion brought a tent, commanding officer, 180lb. This was the largest and, though heavily camouflaged, the most resplendent which was ever mine alone. Not only was there room for the entertainment of friends and for a camp bed (mine had long since followed the 40-pounder tent), but there would have been room for a canvas basin and a hip-bath, to which the same applied. As it was, my non-regimental necessaries could be deployed spaciously. They were the disused Australian bacon tin with wire handle in which my tea was brewed; the bisected kerosene tin which was a rudimentary shower bath when water was available (this was seldom, as was apparent to all who sniffed the tainted breeze), my spinning rod, likewise awaiting water; and a book of verse.

Amid such simplicities life was good. With so little competing for attention, life itself was all that mattered. As it was likely to be short, its enjoyment was the more important. That others were more sumptuously accommodated aroused nothing so sour as envy. There was, for instance, a structure far transcending in glory anything which could ever come my way, and known as a tent, staff sergeant's. This designation includes the beatific community of quartermasters, who naturally live in the style to which they are accustomed. So vital was it that no thought of social injustice should threaten their morale, their tents actually had stitched-in windows. Through these, iron-featured and gimlet-eyed, the occupants peered out.

Even more spacious, good enough even for Sohrab and Rustum, was the tent, Indian privates. Compared to the British counterpart, the bell tent of happy memory in which only an experienced campaigner could hope to lie down without being lynched by his comrades, this was a maharajah's palace beside a semi-detached. Since it consisted mainly of cavernous gloom, it was also similar to the beer tent which gave rise to these ruminations. The time has come to pitch it.

With a doctor of medicine at one end, and a doctor of music at the other, the supporting of the central pole falls to me until the time comes to re-emerge into the cool of the evening. Meanwhile, other, smaller tents have risen from the ground. The tang of hemp and the smack of mallets roll away the years. Practised eyes assess stretch and verticals. The field, for fleeting moments, is half-way to being that manly thing, a camp.

So much for illusion. Only the tents are real. Time marches on, with no about-turns. We shall hear no Reveille before they are struck.

JULY 1975

PRIVATE EMPIRE

BEARING THE FILES of yesteryear, my annual pilgrimage took me to the box-room. The journey is hardly a rejuvenating experience; up unfrequented stairs and into an atmosphere heavily loaded with intimations of mortality. In the half-light and dead air of that lofty vault, even the past has been immobilised.

Having stowed on their predestined shelves the records of twelve months' uneventful life, what it cost and how it was paid for, my eyes willy-nilly ranged around. They fell on the jetsam of days long gone. Photographs of myself on divers horses briefly reawakened the small glories one survives; my long disused golf clubs bespoke follies committed when young. Goodbye to all that, I was about to say, when an object in a far-away corner made me stop and stare. Prone, unshapely, dustladen, yet in size and outline it gave the kiss of life to deep-sleeping memories. Though long neglected, my valise had been a good, indeed an intimate companion; and now the very word has dropped from the military vocabulary.

What the battle-axe was to the Viking, or the shield to the crusader, such were their valises to officers of this century's wars. Life was not tenable without them. Some saw service in both, acquiring labels as contrasting as Scutari and Calcutta, which they wore like medals. Mine, a mere Second World War tenderfoot among valises, had no claim to prolonged distinction. But it had been camp, study and store-room of all my possessions from the North Cape to the Equator, across the latter twice, half-way round the world and back. Those who have not lived out of a valise have missed a whole dimension of the human pilgrimage.

Made of stout canvas, and bound by huge-buckled straps of rawhide which took years to learn to do man's bidding, the valise was designed to carry all a man might need to fight a war. And, properly managed, it did. In well-conducted units the management was delegated to the batman. Thus he became responsible for nothing less than a corner of the Empire, for such was the valise to its possessor. It carried his blankets, his clothes, his books (few but valuable), letters, a photograph or two, and the sparse chattels of active service, all rolled up together like a suet pudding. Fitted with pouches, overlaps, press studs, ingeniously sited leather thongs and eyelets, it was a hold-all designed by a genius, and imposed its own design for living.

In hard weather one slept in one's valise, unrolled and laced snugly up to the chin. It had a receptacle for spare boots which, a little strangely as it seems now, was also the pillow; and very comfortable it was, to those practised in the art of making it so.

Skilfully packed, a valise could carry real valuables, and keep them safe. Bottles of gin, for example. Mine did a free fall from the deck of a ship to an unfriendly quayside forty feet below. It landed with two Gordons and one Plymouth as good as new.

The matter of what a valise could carry was, of course, balanced by the question of who was to carry the valise, rather more than an easy man-load when packed. It was one to which there was no ready answer, if only because in practice it seldom arose. The longest man-propelled journey a valise normally made was from the point of its latest deployment to the nearest transport.

This was generally accomplished by rolling it, behind its proprietor's back, as if it were a large snowball or, if owned in a wealthy regiment, one of the now fashionable circular hay bales.

Motive power was provided through the ammunition boots of any available personnel. The less reputable of them no doubt thus sublimated their feeling towards him to whom it belonged. All that remained was the small detail of lifting it. This was easy enough to men of enterprise, if on to a vehicle. But the problems of loading a valise on to a mule deserve, indeed may well have had, a volume of the Field Service Pocket Book to themselves.

Mules, as a community, are strong on restrictive practices. The mere sight of a valise called into play their vast resources in obstructive techniques. They objected less to its weight than to its size, clumsiness and lack of balance, which made it ill-adapted to loading on a pack-saddle. By the time we reached animal transport basis, most of us had shed or lost so many of our previously treasured possessions that our valises, like ourselves, were unarguably slimmed. This was not a point which a mule would be likely to concede. However, it was one of modest pride to us.

The valise proclaimed a distinction in Army life. It marked out those who were going places from those who were staying places; those who froze or sweated from those (as was written of brave Kempenfelt) whose fingers held the pen. The latter on their peregrinations from one headquarters to another, proclaimed their role by being suitcase men. Indeed I knew some who went to war brief-case in hand.

They struck no envy from me. The bulbous form of my valise, ungainly as it was, a kind of Falstaff among baggage, was better company on which to look back than the most elegant of streamlined travel goods. Up in the box-room my mind's eye could still see it in its prime, when in truth it was my home and all else beside, even when my other eyes could see only its modern self, deflated in old age, fading away in the dim light of the extreme upstairs.

FEBRUARY 1981

BETWEEN THE LINES

FROM THE PUNJAB, a letter. Times were when this would have been unremarkable. Now it was an event. It was an uncommonly pleasing letter. The writer knew England. He thanked me for reminding him, week by week, of scenes, sounds and smells he had known here and 'come to love as part of myself'. He did not wish to exchange his native land for mine. But he did wish to remember, and I had helped to make memory easier.

How well I know the feeling. Far away, our moist air over fallen leaves, if recollected in tranquillity, has fragrance as rare as that of frangipani revived in memory here. What do we know of England, who only England know? Here was somebody in a position to know plenty and to be thirsty, as it were, for a hair of the dog which had bitten him.

In his dusty city, or in the baking plains around it, the nights will now be cold. He will be thinking of English houses at log-fire time, of wet wind and rain, of the common denominator of mud in village lanes, relishing the cheer which once he shared and which we reserve for dark days as autumn slides downwards into winter. Those who fall in love espouse the worst as well as the best, so I do not believe he would be thinking only of village cricket matches on summer afternoons.

It was a short step to playing the game in reverse. If my writing had re-awakened England for him, his postmark had brought old India alive for me. Old India is any India, including modern India. India changes slowly – not much between the time of Christ and our own time in most of the endless villages of that huge land. Some things may have altered in the three decades since I left them but, again, not much.

At the end of an Indian day the sloping sun lengthens the shadows. Across the dun plain the lines of cattle wend back towards the village. Smoke curls upwards in still air, laced with the hot and angry spices that tell of supper. It is a moment of peace unexcelled anywhere in the world; a moment for that deep-running undercurrent of common-sense which dictates Indian life. A day is over; it is time for families to reassemble. And they do. Human experience, which Indians accumulate from a limitless past, keeps the fifth commandment well observed.

After a night of croaking frogs, jackal cries and fireflies the sun will rise on another Indian day. Tall clouds, stacked in a wide sky, will sail across the Punjab plain towards the home of the gods in the Himalaya. Below them mynahs will mimic the men around them, kites wheel in the sunshine and parched crows with beaks agape wait for the respite brought by dusk. Men and women garbed in the colours which here look lurid in our half-light, but are glorious in the Indian brilliance, come and go. The endless crowd, that everlasting omnipresent crowd always passing to its unknown destination like humanity itself and personifying eternal India, recalls *The Pilgrim's Progress*. The young and comely, the old and wizened go wagging along together, whence and whither no man knows.

Theirs is a land, and a life, with an alpha and an omega beyond our understanding. Presumably they think the same of our people, in our interlude of bewilderment while we seek a destiny, each of us seeking to solve the problems of the nation and few of us minding our own business, in the best and most literal sense of that term. Once linked, now separated by half the world, our two races may have no profound lessons for each other, but are surely the better for knowing each other. This, on a wider scale, we continue not to do, except in rare instances.

We live in an age of unprecedented travel. Millions of every nation annually overspill the seas and frontiers, mostly with no other aims in view than to stand and stare in some other country, return home and forget. In this way the wonders of the world become common currency, nations shrink to a common baseline. The world indeed still has its wonders. It was a marvellous place – before the statesmen and politicians made a mess of it, as they have unquestionably done in our lifetime – and could be so again. The letter from the Punjab brought me a message between its lines.

NOVEMBER 1980

Prospect North

We talk much of Scottish magic. For many English people, a year is incomplete without a visit to Scotland. From these four essays some of the reason emerges. The bareness of the Scottish scene, and the minimal mercies of the weather, give a clear view of the sanity of family life, often lost in the sophistication of the south. Perhaps in addition there is a magneticism in the north which attracts men and women as surely as compass needles.

THE FAR COUNTRY

SCOTLAND STEALS UPON the incomer gently. There is no sudden moment of arrival. Even when the eye and the heart have both been straining for the Border, the crossing itself means little. For me A1 is still the Great North Road, and hence less squalid than a motorway. So our passage into the northern kingdom was as magical as ever this year; and as predictable. It was a slow working out of what is more than merely a journey. Hours earlier and a century of miles ago, the long plain of York had run out in the Durham foothills. Grey-blue to the left, the Pennines briefly loomed closer, then retreated, and were succeeded by the Cheviots. To the right, the North Sea sparkled. Herring gulls and kittiwakes patrolled inland from the cliff-tops near Berwick. The bare word, Scotland, apologetically painted on a mundane little bridge, passed almost unnoticed.

Then the Cheviots fell behind. The Lammermuirs took their place until, with Moorfoot intervening, we could see the haze of Edinburgh – still Auld Reekie, even in the smokeless age – with the Pentlands sharp against the evening light beyond. We stopped to tank up at a wayside filling station in the cool of evening. The attendant spoke broad Yorkshire. He was a reminder, in that soft scene amid the rosebay, of England's gritty hardness now behind us, and of the different way of life ahead for the next three weeks. Confirmation came in different tones even as he counted the change.

It is always the first whaup which announces Scotland. That wild free cry means more than maps and road signs. This time he came steadily out of the darkening sky, cried twice more, and was gone. We knew now where we stood. Next day, in lively Scots weather, we crossed firths and mountains in a manner which insulted beauty and history. Forth, Ochil, Tay, Cairngorm, Moray . . . the names slipped by like reproaches for not stopping. But journey's end and its sequel could not be delayed. So we came again, with a sense of discovery unstaled by many previous arrivals, to the land which has given much to the world, but disdained to take much back.

Outwardly Scotland has her own being. It owes nothing to man or to art. The late summer sun rises crimson in the mist, the heather blazes through the day, dusk falls in a violet light and northern air is soft on the face. Wherever the eye ranges it can fall on countryside which is lonely but seldom empty. Inwardly Scotland keeps her spirit. The castles, defying time as they long defied foes, reflect past glories, past valour, past treachery. The proud regiments, the clans, the tartan and the pipes keep the heritage alive. But all of them are the consequence of the Scottish spirit, not its cause.

This year the Scottish way transcended by a yet wider margin the impedimenta of the non-Scots' view of Scotland. All the affectionate folklore about whisky and haggis and tight-fistedness, even the grouse and the salmon and the stags, seemed less important than the central truth of Scottishness, because this was under threat. Daunted by a new and quite unprecedented prospect of prosperity, Scots fear for their peace and their values. This fear was expressed repeatedly during the ceremony of strupach and dram in which stay-at-home Scots bare their souls. And there, away in the simplicities of farm towns and glens, it was impossible not to see their point. There, for all to see, is what much of England has lost. Families stick together. Their young are clean, good-looking, well-mannered and content. Everybody works; nobody hurries. All are friends. It matters little that drinking, when it happens, is a very serious business. Kirk and ceilidhe are both sequels to duty.

The question asks itself why Scotland should be thus blessed. Perhaps the reason is that this is indeed a far country; far from the rat-race; far from dehumanized cities with their envies and recriminations. Small wonder, as the rigs grow and rumours multiply and globe-trotting oil families move in, that material wealth should be eyed with suspicion. Those Scots who seek it emigrate to find it and, having found it, generally let down their roots in foreign soil. Settled round the globe, they represent a twentieth-century diaspora from Toronto to Brisbane and back. Theirs must have been a difficult homeland to leave. Having, as a stranger, made my latest pilgrimage, I marvel that so many stay away.

SEPTEMBER 1974

BEGINNING THE DAY

FROM MY WINDOW in Scotland four human figures meet the eye when, at about seven each morning, I draw the curtain to see what like of a day it is. Two of them are scarecrows. Only after checking their bearings can I be wholly sure which of the four are the neighbouring crofters. Their blocky figures, clad in faded blue boiler suits, may be anywhere about their fields. What is unthinkable is that they will be moving. This is the hour of stillness. Obviously they must move to have left their steadings, and to return again. But to see them doing so is one of Nature's rarest sights.

Willie stands immobilized for a timed 20 minutes after letting out his hens. In that time I bath, shave and dress. He contemplates his flock. His great bronzed hand has not shifted its grip on the feed bucket handle. His brown bald head still lines up with the haycock behind him. Doubtless he moves an inch or so in some direction; but not more. Jamie props his elbows on a dry-stone wall to look his beasts. His ample posterior adds to the landscape a feature best described as rock solid. There he stays while the odours of breakfast coffee waft upwards, and I can look no longer.

Not that I am fool enough to suppose that they waste their time. Each head will be far from empty. Having turned all relevant factors over in his mind, Willie must ken fine which bird is next destined for the pot. Jamie's brain will be full of arithmetic, of which steers are due for mart, and what the margins may be. Both shall surely be right in terms of maximum advantage and minimum disadvantage. Morning is the time to make decisions, and they are best reached in tranquillity. The rest of the day is available for the lesser matter of carrying them out.

Of course the Highlands offer opportunities for tranquillity unexcelled elsewhere. Perhaps this is why the larger world ticked better when statesmen and politicians spent a month or two each year in these parts. A mind made up in the morning calm may well be better so than one bustled about in airports, and limousines to and from No. 10. Mankind in general prefers a slow start to the day and in this differs from womankind. From the moment when women step crisply laundered into public view they perform at full operational efficiency. Not so us men. In me, and apparently in most of us, is a strong element of Willie and Jamie, but with seldom the chance of indulging it to their extreme lengths. Under my own roof far south in Wessex I ask but one thing on waking. It is that nobody, not even my nearest and dearest, shall speak to me for the first hour. Small chance indeed that this should happen. My family have a capacity for sleep (especially after daybreak) which makes a dormouse seem insomniac.

Perhaps there are supermen who in that fresh prime stride purposefully about, getting things done, telephoning people, and in general behaving like women. Not I. With my early tea at hand I sit in peace and cultivate that valuable thing, a complete mental vacuum. In the space thus created constructive thoughts may form. After 20 minutes or so (the Willie and Jamie time-scale) I shower and shave. What more significant moment than that in which the soap is sloshed on in great hot dollops and the day ahead, until now a confused miasma, begins to assume shape, proportion and priorities?

If a day is worth living, or a thing worth doing, it is worth starting slowly so that the best may come of it. That unrivalled occasion for the measurement of self against the everlasting, a day's stalking, exemplifies this. However far the march, no man strides out in the first mile. So give to me, indeed give us all, peace at the start. In worldly terms Willie and Jamie may not have much. But they have this. The great, hot dollops being now dispersed, it is time to check their progress.

Both are now in different places. I bet nobody saw them move. To see a crofter change position before the dew is up is like waiting for a gecko to cross an Indian ceiling. One becomes aware of it only after it happens. Jamie has come to rest amid his barley stooks. One hand is on a sheaf-top, perhaps crumbling away the awns to judge how many days before they stack. Willie is frozen like Lot's wife, scrutinizing a calf. For his sake, I hope it proves golden.

AUGUST 1976

INTO HARBOUR

ONE THICK-SHOULDERED figure, jersey-clad, leans on a bollard. On the outer mole herring gulls take turns to yodel. Men pick at nets on the decks of dozing trawlers. Nothing much is happening round the ribs of a half-built vessel above the slipway. Such is the way of harbours. Little seems to occur. There is nowhere on earth like them for those who, having lost the habit, wish to be reinforced with the *sans souci* spirit.

Being an unashamed, indeed enthusiastic landlubber, deaf to the call of the sea, a harbour is as near to the rolling main as ever I wish to go. Most of our island race may feel invigorated by a bucking deck and the song of the wind in the shrouds. I admire their hardihood, wish them the joy of such things, and a safe return. To pretend to share their pleasure would be to lie. Each to his taste is the governing principle. Inappropriate as it may seem in a presumed descendant of the Vikings, I would rather fall from a horse than drown. To perish in an element not one's own would be an incongruity, as well as unfortunate. So give to me the good earth underfoot; or else at times the rock. Let me be surrounded on every side by hill, vale and forest. Spare me too much sight of that supreme negation, the sea, useful to me only to swim in. Whatever its riches, and they are great, it transcends all deserts as the world's greatest emptiness.

This does not alter the lesson of experience that when a man has nothing to do, a harbour is the ideal place in which to do it. One can be sure of kindred spirits. All present, whether backgrounds be maritime or terrestrial, will be united in this opinion. The knowledge has often stood me in good stead. Little Coramandel ports, where to be stranded is not far short of paradise, exhale the oneness of the human race. The smells of crabs' claws, salt-caked rope, sun-hot canvas, open bilges and drying spars fuse into the scent of ships at rest. In the eternal verities of harbour life, only the temperature differentiates Vizagapurtam from Tromso in the Arctic.

Tromso, where the sealers tie-up and their crews step gingerly ashore, uncertain at first in the treacherous stability of land. To them it is an unfamiliar environment, lifeless and inert, its horizons strangely constant, demanding as much caution as a moon-walk all the short way from gang-plank to bar. So too do the small brown trader captains tread the soil of India as they leave their sailing schooners, those ships from the past which are wonderfully beautiful because the hands that made them had inherited the grace of generations.

Where else to go on the Oman coast, when life has neither urgency nor prospect of immediate change, than the nearest harbour. It is seldom far. There one may lean on a wall, an ear cocked for a phrase in a tongue one knows, and watch the sponge divers sort their haul. Sometimes a longshoreman passes with a bucket of boiling tar. Over all lies the tang of salt and bygone fish, pressed out by the steady heat.

Little is otherwise here, on the rim of Britain's North. All that meets the eye is blue sea, blue sky, tawny rocks, white sand, and the reek of smoking haddock. The mixture is similar the whole world over. The differences of ten thousand miles are lost among the constants. The bollard-leaner puffs his pipe. His is so constant a figure that one speculates which came first, he or the bollard. Did he succeed to it and make it his own? Or did his friends observe him walking with an increasing list, and install the bollard to prevent him keeling over? Idle thoughts in an idle hour, and appropriate to harbours in the summer.

This hasteless, quiet place is not always thus. The time will come again for the crawling sea to rise with the wind behind it, smiting and shattering on the outer mole, showering spindrift where now the dozing trawlers lie. Then the herring gulls will take refuge by riding the tossing air, crying of the wilderness beyond. We need not recall the legend of the voices of dead sailors. The message is plain enough without it.

Nobody can know the welcome of this little harbour except the men who sail into it, even though then they find no sun trap, but a cold and grey shelter, where icy rains bounces off shining oilskins, and the sea roars on outside. How they voice their thanksgiving is their affair, not a landlubber's business. They know the score, and they, not I, have earned this long, hot, lazy day.

September 1976

CROFTING FOLK

BEYOND THE GRAMPIANS lie the crofting counties. If any word can conjure up in one utterance all that is essentially Scottish, that is it. The croft is soul and shrine of the nation. That only a minority of Scots live in, on, or by a croft, or have ever done so, matters little. More than castles and clachans, or any feature of the social spectrum between, crofts provide the setting where the national spirit can be kept muscled up. They set the tone.

By providing a full-time home but a part-time occupation for their inhabitants, crofts impose on their occupants the need for team spirit and all-round competence. Everybody is habitually standing-in for everybody else. Life must go on, outwardly as well as inwardly, and the tasks it imposes are the same no matter who is present or absent.

When the boat goes out, taking the man to his lobster pots, the cow must still be milked – even if the bus has gone, too, because it is shopping day, taking mother in it. So the eldest quine will do the job; or, failing her, the next oldest. Right on down the line through byre and kailyard on the croft itself, those few acres of crop which distinguish a crofter from a cottar, the generations pitch in shoulder to shoulder. A bairn able to toddle can also feed hens and pick up eggs. A loon, no disparaging term, with O-levels can pitch bales or set tatties. Grandfathers stack peat, and so ad infinitum. These are not mere tasks, but responsibilities. They are interchangeable and undodgeable, there being neither demarcation disputes nor overtime on a croft. The principle of life is that whatever needs to be done, all can do and in the end will have to. Hence the mutual reliance which eliminates the us-and-them syndrome from Scottish parents and children.

It is a harder life than that of the towns, but not as hard as it was. No longer is it hungry. Most people have money enough in northern Scotland nowadays, especially since the oil. The traditional formula that farming plus fishing equals crofting is less general than it was. The man (that local simplicity which means exactly what it says, but so much more completely than elsewhere) combines his crofting with wider backgrounds since better communications brought the tourists in, leaving some of their money behind, broadening life and speeding it up. He drives a smart car nowadays when he leaves for work as a roadman, garage hand, lorry driver, school-master, in distillery or quarry or, of course, on the rigs. His family live differently too.

The bright lass who cashes cheques in the bank goes home to feed the calves. A more than usually youthful ghillie not only knows his river, but at other times reads physics at a university down south. Nobody sits around, interrupting the cash flow to a croft. On it or off it, everybody works though nobody hurries. Inside, the way of life reflects this. There is comfort where, traditionally, it was lacking. The latest in television sets looms large. Carpets, decorations, furniture are very different from the expectations raised by outward view.

When the rich and spreading fields of Aberdeenshire fall behind us, and we cross the pass into the lost land of the Cabrach, with great vistas of the true North spreading ahead, the scattered crofts set the tone of more than the landscape. Built of native rock, they merge into it almost invisibly, except for the blowing lines of washing which proclaim their presence like flags. The practised eye can pick them out, assessing the morale of the old friends within from the state of the little squares of oats and barley which, if luck lasts until November, may still be harvested.

Squat-built to lie under the wind, grim-looking from their granite walls, they cling like barnacles to the hard hills, concealing the warmth and light of the life under their roofs. They defy, too, the harshness of surrounding Nature, for no economic improvement alters that old enemy, the Highland winter. When booming winds bring in the snow, and roads are choked (all northern Scotland can count on that) the siege will begin again.

Then the combination of team spirit and self-reliance meets its test. There are more resources now than the turf pile, the tattie heap and the meal sack which represented the means of life in the well-remembered past. But the reality of the survival months is still something which the summer visitor cannot know. The telephone (if there is one) will produce an ambulance, or a rescue party, in emergency. But in mere illness the doctor cannot get through. Nor can shops be reached. The family unit sees it through alone, on its own resources.

The croft is a way of life. It is also a way of facing life. It has produced from the small Scottish nation a proportion, far greater than that in those more numerous, of men and women of worth and competence in the wider world. They have not developed their capacities by being organised, herded and cared for, but by knowing from birth onwards that, no man being an island, he must stand up for himself. And a family must expect to be one.

AUGUST 1980

Night's Dark Face

Darkness and light occupy a near-equal total of hours across the year. But the night as a familiar, visible entity is seldom described. We see sunset as a falling curtain, and regard the scene as closed until dawn. But life goes on. There is as much to see in darkness as in light, sometimes with curious inversions and unexpected truths.

QUEEN OF THE SKY

UNTIL STORMS ENDED her reign, the harvest moon crossed the sky in special glory. Now we are in an interregnum. The hunters' moon follows, but not yet. The moon's varied guises have given her feminine gender. The sun is constant, and by common usage masculine. The moon alters her image as the months pass. To us, earthbound unless we are astronauts, she presents different faces for different seasons.

For harvest she has a gentle brightness. Some of the reasons are obvious. In most years, certainly in this one, the land is dry, humidity low, the atmosphere clear. Nothing dims the luminance of her secondhand sunshine; nor does anything add to it, as will later the reflections from frost and snow. Moreover, she shines upon a change of scene. Night dramatizes what in daylight is mundane. Fields lately heavy and fences half-hidden with the ripened crops are now stubble. Moonlight, whitening light tones and blackening dark ones, projects a countryside squared and ruled into a new geometry.

Hedgerow trees cast hard-etched shadows. For some of us these black patches still magnetize the eye. In such dark areas danger lay in war time, now long ago. Beyond the shadows scattered bushes, windrows and bales which escaped the buckrake illustrate another quality of moonlight. In it objects change their shape if intently watched, and only seasoned campaigners can distinguish that which moves from what does not. To the inexperienced, a stick pile can become an armed man. The converse is also true.

High and clear in the empty sky, the harvest moon awoke alertness in me from which there is no escape. That capricious enchantress was infecting with half-imagined menace the innocent vales of southern England. Standing on a sheep-bitten chalk down above my house I wondered why the palely radiant land around me should turn my thoughts to war and not to peace. Then, picking out the far-off skylines and tracks, such a thing seemed less than strange. King Alfred's men had watched wind-twisted thorn bushes on the slopes below, and doubtless some of the newer recruits had seen them turn into armed men – sometimes in imagination, sometimes not. The skeleton of 16 Danes, all beheaded, were dug up less than a mile away and not long since.

A dark scar on the opposite breast of the valley was once the road which the Romans made from Old Sarum to Clausentum, near what is now Winchester. Along it the legionaries followed the eagle. Above it a great earthwork, still obstinately horizontal after 3,000 years, showed where an unknown people had walled themselves in during a time of trouble. To have built with stags' horn mattocks a double line of embankment 12ft high with a circumference of a mile suggests they had plenty of trouble in view. Other eyes than mine had seen in moonlight what I could only imagine. They were far separated from me in time though not in place, and I felt fellow feeling for those long gone with unquiet minds. At that moment they seemed close, thanks to the continued magic of the now trodden moon.

Her beams may distort both vision and thought, but they leave some things clear. A wavering dot in the stubble below was a hare seeking for undersown clover. A barn owl, more than ever ghostly in the brightness, passed on noiseless wings. Not so two ducks; they quacked and swished across the face of the moon. Dane and Saxon, Roman and Briton, watching through the anxious nights, must have seen their forebears pass. On these windy hills nothing much has changed.

It was time to go. A steep track down the lynchets led me safely home. Time had been well spent. Things seen by moonlight have a new perspective, and an extra truth. A chance to stand and stare in the gentle weather of harvest time had been worth creating. And I have made an engagement, which I shall not break, with the hunters' moon. I shall not expect the same soft luminance. Riding high, she will be hard-faced and brilliant, with an escort of frost-bright stars. With her aid I shall again see for miles through the English night, which has changed less than the English day.

SEPTEMBER 1973

SUMMER THUNDER

FOR A LONG hour the sky crashed and mumbled. Lightning scorched the night. Three times the house blacked out as a power line earthed or a fuse blew somewhere along the grid. Spare circuits were switched-in within seconds, and visibility came and went. To end the uncertainty, we turned everything off, drew back the curtains and watched the outer world. The elements gave better entertainment than the television. Besides which, we were praying for rain.

The night was moonless and thick. Between flashes darkness pressed against the panes like plush. Cloud cover cut out starshine. The small reflections and silhouettes, individually imperceptible, which give perspective on most dark nights were obliterated in the blackness. Whether darkness is ever total is a matter of debate. Much may depend on individual eyesight and much on individual capability to use the other senses in giving clues to what the eye cannot see. From indoors, with the other senses negated, the darkness was as total as any I could remember.

We tracked the storm as it circled our valley. First the thunder sounded south of us, then east, then north. For an hour before last light we had watched the build-up between us and sunset. This was a classic anti-clockwise circuit. At first thunder and lightning seemed sometimes together, sometimes apart. The crackling illuminations lit the countryside in differing sectors and we, because even in darkness the eyes are never still, viewed it from differing angles. The effect was magic. A distant hill, topped by a wood, became a sudden vision, clinically distinct and bluish white, and in the same glance vanished. Spring barley lay silver in another flash, bounded by hedges blacker than ever they are by day.

Then the storm took shape and closed upon us. The thunderclaps grew louder. They formed a rhythm with the lightning. Earlier it had not been possible to link light and sound. Now it was. The intervals shortened. A flash that showed the shrubbery yet drained it of colour, a simultaneous crack which sounded like the sky splitting, another flash that showed bullocks complacently cudding, another crack. . . . Since the female of the species is less impressionable than the male she merely said, 'We must surely get rain now,' whereas I went to look at our daughters.

They lay peacefully asleep. The awesome noises overhead, momentarily as loud as gunfire without its disruptive shock, had not superseded Nature's need for rest. Returning to report all well, I collected whisky and soda on the way, and passed one to my spouse. She said: 'Something to celebrate; listen!' Beyond the windows another sound stirred the opacity of night. A growing sibilance, beginning in a whisper and rising to a rush, told us we had that for which we waited.

Rain was falling; falling vertically, as it does from thunder clouds; falling on to soil and lawns and a surrounding countryside which we knew to be parched arid. I opened the window lest we miss the scent of earth revived.

And so to bed.

It was quieter now. Only a mutter growing fainter in the distance, flickers of light on the ceiling growing fainter too, and still the blessed seeping of the rain. By no standard had we undergone a severe storm. It was an ordinary enough English night. And yet it was a relic of something much more vast, and had stirred memories formed by ancestors long dead. The storm had been a replay, though on nearly worn-out tape, of the collisions, explosions, fires and convulsions in which our world was forged. We had heard the loudest remaining echo of creation. Once the replay must have been more vivid and the echoes louder. Our ancestors of two million years ago were that much nearer the evolution of a habitable planet. And that much nearer the stupendous quakes, volcanics and collapses which divided the continents, held back the seas, and trapped the oil and minerals which we now exploit.

Peering from their caves primeval families must have gazed in awe at tremendous happenings which have simmered down into modern thunderstorms, such as we had viewed in tranquillity from an English country house. They had first learned to live with their world's terrors and, by learning, projected to future generations a faith in their safety despite the noises-off. That faith enabled two girls to sleep on regardless, giving no thought to the boom and volley overhead.

MAY 1976

No more rain fell until that which ended the great drought in September.

HIDDEN HOURS

SLEEP WAS IMPOSSIBLE one hot night. Better to give up the long vain wait, to rearrange the pillows, to surrender to consciousness, to look the night in the eye, and to enjoy for a change the hours from two to four in the morning. Apart from those occupationally committed, few of us ever see them.

The windows face south. Beyond them a loom of moonlit down stretched to the blackness of a spinney. Life was going its way unseen and unheard in that half-mile. A half-fledged partridge covey harbour there. Nightly we hear the cock calling the family to jug. Stalking through the savannah formed by the ancient grass would be that miniature panther, a weasel. He had flashed across the track ahead of me at dusk. I wished the partridges luck. Nothing less could save at least one of them; unless, of course, the weasel met a tender young rabbit first. The windows were open. Through their wide gape the breath of night came fresher. I listened for a scream which would spread the news of murder done in the normal course of Nature. Silence reigned.

Silence was surprising. Between me and the spinney at least a million creatures were living out their various patterns of existence, yet not a sound was to be heard. It seemed that the whole world slept, except me. The absolute detachment of the small hours declared itself. Partly because of night's cool breath, partly from a wish to pierce the encircling quiet, I decided to go more closely to it. In my dressing gown I walked the lawn below the window, ears tuned for any break in the conspiracy of silence. The drone of a beetle, the whine of a midge would have been enough. None came.

Summer nights have beauty in negative, clearly toned, but void of colour. In this new idiom, time was needed to relearn sights taken for granted by day. The ash tree which is a wood-pigeon's junction, the cricket field silver instead of green, the shadowless bulk of our own tarred barn, the surprise element of a combine left at a field gate the previous evening, all were new and unfamiliar in that light and at that hour. Up the valley a tide of mist was creeping, shining under the moon. Beyond it a dairy herd grazed, spread across their pasture like troops in open order. The hour would be usual enough to them; of all creatures cows are least in doubt about the time in terms of proximity to the next milking.

The bats which flew as the sun went down were no longer crossing the stars; they, too, had no use for the dead of the night, though dawn would see them out again. No owls called; despite the pressures of feeding a family in midsummer's few dark hours, they found time for a siesta. No headlights swept the sky. Nothing it seemed, moved. But I knew that much did. Foxes would be busy, hares grazing, shrews on those travels in which so many die mysteriously on roads and footpaths, badgers foraging, rats up to no good, to name but a few. In the tight-packed pre-harvest countryside they would do all this unseen, and, it seemed, unheard. Only a long-drawn, contented snuffle from the stables signalized life.

Yet never is the land more crowded than in these weeks after the summer's zenith. Nearly every young bird has fledged. Migrant species are still with us. Winter has yet to take toll of the old and ailing. The bird population must be doubled, and more. The same applies, in lesser degree, to mammals. Insect numbers are multiplied many times above normal. That they go unseen is no mystery. Except for haysels and pasture, crops still cover the land. Hedges, twice their winter width, are curtained and bushed-out by old man's beard, bryony, bindweeds, bramble, bracken, nettle and willowherb. The countryside, glutted with the summer's gains, lay weighed down by the heavy air.

The vapour which had sedimented into mist was now rising again. It reddened the moon, dulled the stars and soaked the lawn in dew. On a day when by breakfast time all would be scanning the skies for rain, the world was sodden before sunrise.

In a heat wave values are reversed. Failing in the quest for sleep, I had found rest only by waking. Men who expect thirst feel hunger instead as they work in the cracked and tawny fields. The night's cool breath had been an illusion. The air hung heavy and windless; even out of doors the heat seemed to pulsate. I went indoors for a shower.

JULY 1975

BATS' FLIGHT

To check that the paddock gate was actually latched, and not merely pushed to, gave good reason for a stroll at nightfall. But it was not the real one. After the summer's first hot day there is balm in the oblivion when dusk has deepened into dark. Then comes the scent of invisible flowers, the peppery fume of dry nettles, and the give-away sounds of unseen countryside. Indignation from a cock pheasant indicated a breach of the peace. From owl to owl some private message went. A scuffling in the hedge was probably a hedgehog too well protected to bother about caution. A far-away cow blared for the bull or an absent calf. There came a chirp overhead as if a finch suffered from insomnia. But the chirper was no finch.

The great horseshoe bats were on the wing again. They live in cracks in the cliff-like face of an ancient chalk pit behind the house. A little earlier I might have seen them patrolling like misshaped jackdaws in the last of the light. Inevitably the whole bat-community shares a sinister, even evil, image. The dead black wings, the figures hunched and hooded in repose, the lives so remote from ours that they are assumed to be inimical, arouse no affection from the human race. But where there is mystery there may also be attraction.

Neither hate nor fear should be aroused by the ubiquitous little pipistrelle. Few countrymen would recognize the name. To them it is the flittermouse, similarly named with variations in spelling across Germanic Europe from the Welsh March to Prussia. The great horseshoe bats are less assuring. They are bigger and more assertive, and for the few who achieve a close-up view, there is shock in their appearance. The face-design, made of naked skin, from which they gain their name, is as hideous and grotesque as a witch-doctor's mask, and a strange origin for so innocent a voice.

Whether they wait for warm nights before sallying forth, or whether I do, remains a mystery to me. But only warmth brings out their favourite prey, the cockchafers and dor beetles and the more substantial moths. All are too large to be eaten on the wing, as the flittermouse swallows its midges. A pear tree outside our bedroom window is the dining hall of the local great horseshoe bats. There they hang themselves upside down, strange, shapeless, indeterminate silhouettes against the stars or moonlight. And there they gibber in the night, against a sonic background of shufflings and flappings, of cracking wing cases, and a general impression of uncleanness.

They remain a source of minor pride to me. Few of us can say that we have held a bat, alive or dead, in our hands. Not all of us who have had this distinction, least of all myself, know much of the great hidden nationhoods of bats the world over. The names of the 12 British species have enigmatic overtones. Only three are recognizable to me. They are the flittermouse, the greater horseshoe, and that dashing and sometimes diurnal figure the noctule. How agreeable to have known just once, not more, some of the others. Does Natter's bat live up to his name? Who were Daubenton, Bechstein and Leisler, who each likewise named a species? Why should the barbarstelle thus be named? So much to know. And yet perhaps I already know sufficient.

Only twice has it been my fate to meet bats at a personal level. It has been enough. Long ago in a chimney in Snowdonia my leader dislodged a sleeping colony which showered down on me in all their repellent fustiness. Not for me to wonder, as they fell onwards into the void beneath, whether they were of any of the species named, or perhaps whiskered bats, or long-eared bats, or Serontines, or any of the others. Presumably they awoke and began flying before they reached the rocks up which we had come. Later in India at a time of dearth, I ate not one, but several. They were fruit bats and excellent, though some indoctrination was required. It happened in hospital, where man acquires the habit of doing what he is told.

'Today,' the nurse had said, 'you will have solid food. Believe it or not, chicken.' I believed it, but not for long. It looked good. It smelled good. Boiled, I diagnosed, and covered with white sauce. Impaling the uppermost layer, I lifted the fork. Bone after interconnected bone reared themselves arm's length above the plate, with apparently more to follow. The nurse bustled urgently to the bedside. 'They should have chopped off that bit,' she said crossly, doing so. 'Now come on; eat up your nice bat.'

What has been done once can be done again. In times like these the great horseshoes may yet come in handy. We are told there is to be a protein shortage.

JULY 1974

BACK TO THE OLD DAYS

NIGHT FALLS EARLY in the dead of winter. Then, in our small village of two hundred souls, darkness follows. This may seem a glimpse of the obvious, but is nevertheless rare in the England of today. We have no street lighting. Indeed we do not have a street in the modern meaning of the word. So there is no need of the artificial illumination which now denies the blessed gift of undiluted night to most of the inhabited countryside.

Here, when day is done and no afterglow shows up the television aerials in silhouette, a subtle change takes place. Except when a car goes through, the village is as bygone generations knew it. No longer isolated in the twentieth century, cut off from history by the all-pervading technology, it moves back into Time, linking up with all that went before.

Darkness is never total. So white walls show dimly beside our five small lanes. The houses, much modernised internally, look outwardly as they must have looked for centuries to breadwinners returning from plough-tail, woodland and workshop. They are scattered in agreeable absence of plan. Though many times re-placed they may reflect the sites and prospect chosen by the Saxon immigrants who settled here fourteen centuries ago. And they, perhaps, followed precedents set by the Iron Age cultivators who preceded them – and who may themselves have built their huts where pre-Celtic flint knappers made their dwellings, and so into the long tunnel of the past beyond the limits of our knowledge.

Men have been coming and going along Great Lane, Sheep Way, Sloe Gate, the Green, and Doggrels while civilisations waxed and waned. Reincarnated and put down here in daylight, those old-timers would be bewildered and lost. In the dark they would surely find their way. Far from obscuring things, darkness concentrates the mind, bringing into play senses other than sight, on which we are over-dependent, and which confuses by presenting us with more information that we can analyse and evaluate. Enclosed in night, our unity is enhanced. Instead of hiding us from each other, it brings us together.

In 300 yards to and from the letter box I learn things which would pass unnoticed in daylight. The farmer upwind has opened his silage. They have had a bonfire behind the inn. The aromatic air from freshly sliced earth and severed roots tell where the main ditch has been cleared. A rectangle of bright light shows for a second or two and vanishes. One cat more is on patrol.

Headlights beyond the crest of the downland road sweep skyward, find the base of low cloud, and remind me of the blitz. Then the car comes over the crest, and follows the curving road downwards to the village. Tree shadows, huge and misshapen, march across walls. We are no longer ourselves alone. An alien presence is invading us. Perhaps it is destined for a house in the village, in which case it will merge into our small world when its lights are switched off.

In the event it does not. It snakes through the village, ascends the hill on the opposite side and travels on, pushing its zone of intrusive luminance ahead of it. Because it did not stop, it becomes a thing of no consequence. It came, temporarily destroyed our self-containment, and went. The village reverts into itself, nearer again to its own long past than to the surrounding present; more aware, once more, of its own small happenings than of all outside its orbit. Gravel, swept down the road by recent rain, crunches under my boots. 'Night!' says a voice behind a garden hedge. 'Goodnight, George,' I answer. 'Oh, 'tis you, then?' 'Indeed it is. Goodnight.' 'Goodnight.'

And there, hidden in our small world, the matter drops. But it seemed important at the time.

JANUARY 1980

THINGS TO COME

THIS HARD WINTER's second ice-age showed me my native land in a new and awesome guise. Menace. One does not expect menace in England, as non-extreme in weather as in the character of her people. And only very rarely does the rest of Britain confront a genuine threat from the elements.

Their message could not be mistaken last month. It was a pitiless and nihilistic scene that confronted me as I drove away from Newmarket towards the refrigerated South-West late one deadened afternoon. The spectacle was unnatural to these islands, though I had met something like it elsewhere. Over the Canadian barrens, when the months-long Polar night is falling, such sights are sometimes seen. Perhaps also they loom above the Russian steppes, calling forth all the fatalism and courage of that enduring people. But what I saw in these gentle islands seemed like an exaggerated dream.

Down the road that leads from the famous Heath to Royston and to sunset, visibility was repeatedly lost in snow glare. Frost-lift had split the surface of the drifts into countless small filaments from which the levelling rays were refracted into a mist of blinding light whenever the road lay directly up-sun. The visor was useless against it. Perhaps not surprisingly, I had no dark glasses. The only course was to brake immediately, and drive at walking pace until the direction veered out of the eye of the sun, steering meanwhile by the line of the verge viewed through the near-side window, and praying that nothing was coming the other way.

Then the sky began to redden. Not only the sky, but the land also. The snow-bound fields which stretched from horizon to horizon reflected the sunset colours, which deepened like a staged effect. This was not the 'red sky at night' of popular fancy. It was a deepening, sullen crimson; awesome in its suggested violence, foreign to that familiar road, it left its message of foreboding, Red for danger, as darkness slowly swallowed the hue of blood. Subconsciously, I took the point. There could be no haste that night, just mile on mile to be prudently harvested, the march of time forgotten. The warning in the frozen sky stayed there for 20 minutes, creating a bizarre fantasy.

Ahead lay the inoffensive towns of Hertfordshire, the route so often traversed that I could visualise its whole length in my mind's eye. I was travelling home. But in that interval the way ahead looked more like the edge of hell, the cold hell of oriental mythology.

Did others also see that violent, ominous sunset and marvel at it? And was it visible to all of Britain, or of local viewpoint only – some optical illusion caused by a trick of light as the solar rays struck freezing vapours above the long-drained fens? I have asked myself the questions since. Perhaps nobody knows. All that I know is that this winter brought an element of malevolence which did not exist in the two comparably hard winters within my memory, 1947 and 1962. The differences were marked.

In those earlier years the country was merely a temporary waste land. This time it suffered actual assault. What happened went so far beyond the limits of reasonable apprehension that reality itself seemed left behind.

That Braemar – innocent, welcoming Braemar, so ideally situated for a tea-break halt and eye-stretching contemplation of the royal Dee – should have been colder than the South Pole seemed typical of distorted proportions and shaken perspectives. We shall remember such grotesqueries while, for months to come, we contemplate the actualities. We shall pay for them, if only via the rates. The roads are an obvious example. As the packed ice turned to slush and drained away, we could see their sorry state. They were not bad roads, back in November. Now they show what the snow ploughs did to them. Axle-cracking potholes yawn where Mr. Macadam himself would have been proud of the surface.

The contraction and subsequent upheaval of the land, caused by weeks of unprecedented cold, split concrete as if it had been land-mined. The infiltration of frost caused roofs to leak. The bills are to come.

But as we look back, it is not this winter's havoc nor its beauty (and there has been some) which dominate the memory, but the fear that it induced. This was both immediate and long-term. It was aroused by both the pre- and post-Christmas snowfalls and their attendant circumstances. A Salisbury Plain farmer, looking for his sheep on the land where he was born, confessed himself physically frightened by the savagery of the first blizzard. Not seriously doubting that he could find his way home, he still felt a sense of being under personal attack, as though the inanimate forces of Nature were uniting against him. Driving home across the ghostly, whitened countryside after that barbaric sunset, I felt likewise as the fog wraiths closed in on the motorway ahead.

Forseeing the future, it seemed that we might be seeing the character of times to come. Never previously do I recall snow retaining its vestal whiteness so long unsullied. Normally snow is messy stuff, soon made scabrous by the dirt amid which it falls. But not this time. White it fell, and white it stayed, the pure and neutral white of lifelessness, as though the snow was demonstrating the superiority over all earthly influences of winter suddenly projected at peak power. Past history tells us how Ice Ages came and went – the Ice Ages that were actual for the North Hemisphere, and not mere figures of speech – and there is no indication that their sequence has ended for ever.

The next one has to start somewhere, sometime. Perhaps the atmospheric pressure-lock which held us in its thrall is not a passing phenomenon, but a balance of natural forces that will be repeated, perhaps indeed become a norm. In which case the daunting impressions left by those cold weeks could be a warning more significant than the harm they did.

FEBRUARY 1982

Here and Hereafter

Those who look much at Nature generally concern themselves with present facts, seldom asking the ultimate Why? But those facts may themselves contain clues to the outcome when that question is put. The disparities of Creation in size, scope, time and distance; the similarities between the experience of one life form and another; the physical certainty about what will one day befall our Earth all tend subtly towards an answer.

WELL SPENT

NOW THE DAY was over, or nearly so, and the more muscular Christians converged upon the church. Our Sundays see the division familiar in most villages. Morning service is for women, white-collar workers, young men and maidens, old men and children. The evening responses are baritone and bass. From the rearmost pew the shoulders and biceps of those in front could be seen bulking up firmly under sober suits. This congregation was laced with tractor drivers, stockmen, builders, woodmen and others of solid physical construction and in the prime of life. Even the ringers emerged from the bell chamber into the church and not out of it, which they would not dream of doing in the morning. Thus it has always been in my memory of three villages. The cause escapes me. But the convention is probably general throughout the Church of England that men, if they attend at all, go to evening service.

Perhaps it was not mortal sin to speculate through Evensong. In that mainly masculine company we did not seem insulated from the main stream of life. It had been a spring day rich enough to make thanksgiving spontaneous. Perhaps some were present for that reason. But most I knew to be regulars.

The sun, now well down the sky, sent a slanting shaft of light across the nave. In it there floated the million motes of dust ever present in every church. From outside came the sounds of the world at large. That is to say, our world; not a big one, but worth living in; worth, also, keeping the way we like it. Cars passed, as did a motor-cycle or two. They slowed, changed down, and accelerated away leftwards at the cross-roads and up the hill at the top of which stands the inn. Opening time is 6.30 there too. There would be those among us, throats parched from having sung unto the Lord a new song, who would in due course walk home that way and gaze down into the cool depths of a pint or two.

The intervals between engines were filled by the medley of blackbirds and thrushes. Another songster, rare in our lean-soiled chalk country, added his voice. I promised myself a stroll after dark. To praise the Lord with trumpets also and shawms was all very well for now, even if only in theory. But it would not do to miss the nightingale's contribution when other voices fell silent and left him the soloist. Silence was still hours away. Cheerful shouts and satisfying smacks indicated cricket practice. The nets had been pitched nearer the church than usual. On reflection it seemed meet and right so to do. In or out of earshot, the thoughts of a summer congregation are seldom far from cricket anyway. And had we been unable to hear bat on ball they could not have heard The day Thou gavest, to which we now did full justice, and from which even the souls of cricketers must benefit.

Wings were clapped and flapped as wood-pigeons came to roost in the yews, swapped places and organized themselves before cooing their way through the sermon. The parson drew a distinction (new to me but none the less welcome) between mean sins and warm-hearted sins. I took the hint to commit more of the latter than the former should total avoidance of both prove impossible. Then there was a jingling of money in trouser pockets as the sidesmen came round during the last hymn.

So we sought that peace which even our tranquil small world cannot give, asked for our darkness to be lightened, and for quiet minds when the shades lengthen, the fever of life is over, and our work done. After that we filed out through the porch into a day whose sun was lower in the sky, whose air was more chilly, and midges more numerous than when we entered. We paused at the lych gate for routine jokes and the filling of pipes. We had not wasted our time.

MAY 1975

HEAVENS ABOVE

MY EYE WAS caught by Betelgeuse on a cold cloudless evening. In icy splendour, stars glowed and glittered from horizon to horizon. Having that rare boon, ten minutes to spare, I stood on the lawn and repaired some friendships. Orion was loping low to the south-east. Never here does he bestride the high sky as he does in the tropics. To see him thence, amd to know that those at home could see him too, was a good thought in hard times to some of us who had acquired this impractical information. In dry clear air far to the east of Suez, individual stars have distinctions lacking in our damp island. But, even here, Betelgeuse, red on the Hunter's shoulder, proclaims himself different from the rest. Indeed, he is. With a diameter of 290 million miles he is big enough, were he hollow, for our earth to circle the sun in its present orbit inside him. Such magnitude and such distance are beyond the benumbed conceiving of such as me. The immensity of creation became an overwhelming thought, interrupted by a crick in the neck.

Impromptu star-gazing is not for those with much-bashed spines. If indulged in, the muscles must be eased occasionally. I eased mine by lowering the angle of sight. This brought me face to face with Sirius. He has a useful distinction. In emergency he may be recognizable independently of his constellation. A fair view of him through a gap in cloud can be enough to identify him even if no other is visible, to the solace of wayfarers and seafarers here below. A diamond brilliance in pulsating colours representing 25 times the luminosity of the sun, establishes him. But this glory is kept for the desert air. Always low in our latitude, his radiance is seldom undimmed by the less clear atmosphere. But now, in still air and frost, Sirius put on a display worthy of a Himalayan winter night. He flashed white and green as if coding a message. The rays that carried it had left him just before the 1966 General Election. It was a pleasing reminder of better times.

The magnificence of half the universe made me ask myself why I stand and stare at it so seldom. Wiser men than I have looked at it long and lovingly since the birth of the human race with every motive from inevitable awe to analytical intelligence. In simpler times than ours, with fewer alternative preoccupations, the world's great backcloth challenged Man's thirst for knowledge. Hence the Arab mathematicians, far ahead of their time in the Roman era. But knowledge was not all, and must never be. Hence also the fascination to less factual men, and mankind's debt for the enrichment of the arts.

By walking round the end of the house it might be possible to have a view of Lyra. The constellation includes Vega, the midsummer star which inspired Richard Jeffries. Less than a week from Christmas, Vega was hard to find. Of course, I should have known.

Lyra lies low to the North in winter. Demoted from the zenith where he is expected, Vega looked insignificant. Not so those faithful stands-by, the Plough, Cassiopeia and the Pole Star. They dominated the night in bold familiarity. The Pleiades were outshone. They come to view less readily in best visibility, when rivals otherwise unnoticed are seen round this beguiling little group which reminded Job of his place in the scheme of things.

For I was doing what men have done in all ages, replenishing my stocks of those components in life-style which run short from time to time. Wonder, humility and reverence all grow in the presence of the stars and in the realization of some simpler truths about them. To imagine the universe is impossible without looking at them in silence and solitude. This limitless reality passes understanding. One cannot yet explain it by science, only by guess and by God. With the evidence before me, I prefer God.

A door opened. A daughter came out. 'What are you doing?' she asked. 'Looking at the stars,' I answered. 'Coo, there's millions of them,' she said. There are. Her time will come to spend part of a frosty night posing that unanswerable, Why?

JANUARY 1974

WINGS OF THE MORNING

SEVEN O'CLOCK, AND the hill track is full of life. Three dilatory rabbits have been watched away homeward-bound by the spaniels. A dusting partridge interrupted his ablutions. A butterfly procession is in full swing. Soon the day will be too torrid for watching, so we make the most of the cool. My sub-teenage daughter moves ahead beside a rut deep cut by tractor wheels, amid cornflower, oxeye, ragwort, nettle, hardhead, bindweed, bramble and dog-wood. I follow, spotting from greater height the things worth seeing. The spaniels follow me, foreseeing no advantage for themselves and making no secret of their non-enthusiasm. Westerly air comes upward along the line of the track. The track is itself a line of flowers between two deserts of ripe barley. So the nectar drinkers meet us face to face.

A six-spot burnet hovers on invisible wings, a miniature humming-bird sipping at the cups of cornflower. Purple hairstreaks slip between the bramble clumps. We see meadow browns, small heaths, chalkhill blues, skippers, tortoisehells, a comma, and once, glory be, the bright tawny wing and athletic flight of a silver-washed fritillary, downwind of its native wood. Not for years has there been such a butterfly summer. The best is yet to be. At apple-picking time, when the nymphalidae fly in strength, and the red admirals and painted ladies seek a change from rotting windfalls, the buddleia will offer sights transcending anything man-made. The years fall away. For once manhood has provided the equal of anything remembered from boyhood.

But manhood cannot be cast off. A spinning ball is on its way, of the kind which must be expected by those senior enough to walk before breakfast with a sub-teenage daughter. A straight bat is called for. There can be no padding-up when the young ask questions. This one, destined to go to the heart of so many matters, at first seems simple. 'Does a butterfly know that it used to be a caterpillar and does a caterpillar know when it goes to sleep that it will be a butterfly when it wakes up?'

This is no moment to opt out; unless one does not mind being opted out of other matters than the cognition range of lepidoptera. So an issue-dodger such as 'Well, we can't ask it, can we?' would be less clever than it might seem. Solon should be living at this hour. But he is not. I must do the best I can. My hypothesis is that the caterpillar does not know, if only because none of us know when we go to sleep just how we shall awaken, or even that we shall awaken at all. We merely expect to. Our expectation is faith based on experience. In the unlikely event of a caterpillar having faith, its experience can only be terrestrial and pedestrian, providing no grounds to envisage free, far-ranging life in another element, let alone in another form.

Nor is remembrance by the butterfly likely. Even if it were possible, no butterfly would believe it. Comparing its colours and its mobility with the grotesque dissimilarities of its earthbound earlier being, a butterfly could only dismiss the proposition as absurd. Reproving me in youth for what he thought the unnecessary shooting of a crocodile, an elderly philosopher in the Sunderbands opined that I might have been a crocodile myself in an earlier passage through the world. At the time I thought him a little cracked; now I am less sure. Preposterous though it seemed, a crocodile re-existing as a man would be no more preposterous than the idea of a caterpillar turning into a butterfly, if we did not know by long-established proof that this happens.

After my condensed version of these findings, conversation drifted to other subjects. We walked home. The species seen were entered in the notebook. But this mystery of life, so fortuitously presented, would not be forgotten.

Every caterpillar lays itself away, entombed or hidden, in advance of the great alteration during which the chrysalis comes so closely and so significantly to resemble a mummy from an Egyptian grave. The parallel comes very near to the great enigma of the human race. Chrysalis or winding sheet, is there a difference except in timing? From one, life in a new form will eventually emerge; from the other, life has already gone and nobody yet knows that it does not take new form. There is no reason to suppose it any less existent than the life of the butterfly stretching its wings to the sun.

Those who profess pre-emptive disbelief in individualities continuing after our trip through this world must be gullible as well as unobservant. For one thing is certain. Life goes on. And there is nothing very surprising about sleepers who do not know how they will wake.

JULY 1976

BLAZE OF GLORY

WE WHO LIVE on a dying star have a vested interest in Nature's recessionals. Now another has joined the march into the past. A single gale is enough. One night's hard blow, stripping the leaves long ready to go, wipes out the gorgeous hues of autumn.

The next dawn discloses the neutrality of winter. We have seen it before; we shall, God willing, see it again; and this year we have had more weeks than usual in which to contemplate the country in full majesty.

From September, when the chestnut leaves turn golden, we watch the colours gather. Beech woods turn rusty, then fiery. Oak leaves take the complexion of old ale, and fade to yellow. Elms shower brittle orange leaves to gather in the furrows while their whirling keys fly further but seldom root. Sycamore, hornbeam, maple, birch and alder add their splashes of colour. Only the ash, that most gracious of trees, has nothing to add.

Every year the wonder of retraction grows. The symbolism grows too. Those who are young give their hearts to spring. It is the season of transience, as is human youth, and is greeted with pleasure sharpened by the knowledge that it will not last. Neither will autumn, but one wishes it would. What will follow is not so beguiling that we hasten to embrace it.

Meanwhile, summer has come and gone. Artificer-man has made summer a holiday season. Nature does not, and natural man cannot afford to. Summer is the time of peak production by every growing thing, and therefore the time of peak endeavour by those who are still living naturally. The human race, like all animate creation, remains parasite on the world of plants – and harvest is the great predation. When the countryside dons the livery of achievement and maturity in preparation for retirement, mankind is linked to the rhythm. Life flows. Life ebbs. A closing magnificence is part of the design.

Knowledge has not solved its mystery. We have learned how to blow up the world and walk on the moon, but we still do not know why we are here; nor what other forms and impulses Life may involve which are temporarily imperceptible to us. Although scientists may one day create Life in the sense of a laboratory achievement, it will be surprising if they are led thereby to define its extent and potential. Only experience can do that. Perhaps (as many believe) experience is not to be finalized in one lifetime.

When autumn passes into winter, plant life withdraws, drawn back into the earth where, by processes understood by us, it awaits the moments for resurgence. Not yet understood by us is the application of a similar process to ourselves. Common sense suggests that a parallel exists. From the formlessness of youth men grow to their destined fullness. Life, with its aspirations, and its sensitivities, brings humanity as well as trees to full magnificence as the moment of departure approaches. I cannot say, 'Change and decay in all around I see' when I look on autumn. Ripeness, fulfilment and certainty are more evident.

How many more? Luckily, none can say. Equally luckily, we can remember the beauties of the one just ended. They were, as always, beauties which included promise. The death of Earth, in the sense of the cessation of the possibility of life upon it, may be millions of years away, and probably is, if man forsakes his foolish ways. But it is certain that the eventuality will at some time be reached.

That, to say the least of it, will be an interesting time to be alive. It is a pleasant hope, if only an idle conceit, that this troubled but beautiful world may live up to each autumn's promise and end in a blaze of glory.

NOVEMBER 1972

Also available in Unwin Paperbacks

COME DAWN, COME DUSK

Norman Mursell

Few gamekeepers are better qualified than Norman Mursell, with fifty years experience behind him, to write about the arts of his profession – rearing birds, dealing with vermin, exciting and dangerous encounters with poachers, working with dogs, and so on – but *Come Dawn, Come Dusk* is much more than a gamekeeper's manual. It carries the unmistakable authenticity of the countryman writing about the countryside he knows and loves, and painting a picture in which its wildlife, its farming, its customs, characters and crafts all take their place. The effect is greatly enhanced by Rodger McPhail's delightful drawings.

'a gem...full of atmosphere, not only of the great estate but of a way a new generation of shooting men can never experience except through the work of a man such as Norman Mursell.'

Country Life

GREEN AND PLEASANT LAND

Norman Mursell

In this book, Norman Mursell turns his attention to the ways of the country village and its people. He writes of their celebrations, such as roasting an ox on Coronation Day and the annual 'Wakes', of everyday cottage life fifty years ago, of village politics, of weddings and funerals, of the village church and the village pub. Above all he writes with humour and affection of the village characters – all-rounders like 'Watty' Huxley, expert hedger, long-jump champion, bandmaster and grower of record-breaking vegetables, and leaders of the village community like Tom ('the Cornerstone') Broster.

As in *Come Dawn, Come Dusk*, Norman Mursell's writing is illuminated by Rodger McPhail's exquisite drawings.

IN A GREEN SHADE
Richard Mabey

Reflecting on this selection from his writings on countryside and landscape over the last ten years Richard Mabey has written: 'I began to recognise not just recurrent preoccupations...but a common focus round which all the pieces, to one degree or another, revolved. What they seemed to be searching for was a contemporary redefinition of the country side, and of our relationships with its natural life. What were we trying to get out of it, particularly those of us who neither lived nor worked there? Where was "there" for that matter?'

The book begins with some highly personal accounts of the author's 'own' corners of Britain: Hertfordshire and East Anglia. Then there are forays into the New Forest, the Yorkshire Dales and to a strange area of tidal woodland in Cornwall. Other essays touch on the pure pleasure to be gained from reading maps, on the botanical marvels to be found on some of London's rubbish tips, on the wildlife of Hyde Park and the natural history of Oxford and on such major country writers as Gilbert White and Richard Jeffries.

John Ebdon

EBDON'S ODYSSEY

A chance encounter set John Ebdon on a single-handed expedition to the Cyclades. There he fell irretrievably in love with the country, the island people and their way of life.

This brilliant, often very funny, account of his adventures in the islands of Andros and Kos is concerned with people, primarily the men and women of two villages in the islands but also with fellow countrymen who blundered into his life there.

EBDON'S ILIAD

A return to Greece and to Kos in the Cyclades sets John Ebdon on a fresh round of adventures – funny, sad, ridiculous and poignant.

This book, like *Ebdon's Odyssey*, is about people: The Proper Young Woman and Knickers-to-Match, who invade his mid night accordion music or disturb his musings at the Taverna, and also the islanders Stephano, the irrepressible lecher, the long-suffering Klimi and the indomitable Mama Barbunia.

THE FIRST CUCKOO: A Selection of the most witty amusing and memorable Letters to *The Times* since 1900

Revised edition

Kenneth Gregory

The first edition of witty, entertaining and memorable correspondence to *The Times* was greeted with great critical enthusiasm and went on to become a best-seller. Now Kenneth Gregory has revised his selection of the most witty, amusing and memorable letters to *The Times* since 1900. Among the 'top people' whose eloquence fills these pages figure a host of writers, artists, sportsmen, statesmen and public personalities. There is Conan Doyle on a military intervention, Neville Chamberlain on the grey wagtail, Winston Churchill on corporal punishment and letters on toads, tea-boys, triremes, gnomes, postage stamps, British Rail, chamber-pots, knitting, foreigners and trade unions – from correspondents as diverse as Kenneth Clark, Beverley Nichols, Professor Hayek and Graham Greene. And of course more about the sighting of the first cuckoo in Spring.

THE SECOND CUCKOO: A Further selection of witty, amusing and memorable Letters to *The Times*

A totally new selection of letters to *The Times* – among them ones by Evelyn Waugh on earning an honest dollar, Sir Thomas Beecham on tempo, Reginald Bosanquet on Army nicknames, Patience Strong on 'God Save the Queen', Marie Stopes on pocket money, Agatha Christie on Shakespeare, Joyce Grenfell on 'glamoramas' and many, many more.

This time Kenneth Gregory has been able to include running correspondence on trouser turn-ups, the origin of marmalade, the whereabouts of Ruritania, hygiene and the Communion cup, military nicknames and perfect manners – and cuckoos ã la Beethoven.

AMAZING TIMES!: A Selection of the most amusing and amazing articles from *The Times*

Stephen Winkworth
Illustrated by ffolkes

The kangaroo which stole a five pound note, the soldier who stowed his girlfriend in his kitbag, artificial icebergs, the penicillin black market in Berlin, the golden eagle which travelled in a laundry basket, how the Vatican was invaded by white ants, the elephant that water-skied, the couple who lived in a tree, the 101-year-old lady who slid down banisters, the curry which turned a girl pink...Add to that Lucky Luciano's funeral, the last days of Nijinsky, Casanova's autobiography, Picasso's painting machine, the curse of the Hope diamond and the founding of the Order of the Mosquito... and you have *Amazing Times!*